my **revisi🔆n** notes

AQA A-level
PHILOSOPHY
PAPER 1 EPISTEMOLOGY AND MORAL PHILOSOPHY

Jeremy Hayward
Daniel Cardinal
Gerald Jones

HODDER
EDUCATION
AN HACHETTE UK COMPANY

Orders: please contact Bookpoint Ltd, 130 Park Drive, Milton Park, Abingdon, Oxon OX14 4SE.
Telephone: +44 (0)1235 827827.
Fax: +44 (0)1235 400401.
Email education@bookpoint.co.uk
Lines are open from 9 a.m. to 5 p.m., Monday to Saturday, with a 24-hour message answering service. You can also order through our website: www.hoddereducation.co.uk

ISBN: 978 1 5104 5197 1

© Jeremy Hayward, Daniel Cardinal, Gerald Jones 2019

First published in 2019 by
Hodder Education,
An Hachette UK Company
Carmelite House
50 Victoria Embankment
London EC4Y 0DZ
www.hoddereducation.co.uk

Impression number   10 9 8 7 6 5 4 3
Year   2023   2022   2021   2020

Cover illustration by Barking Dog Art

Illustrations by Barking Dog Art

Typeset in India by Aptara Inc

Printed in Spain

A catalogue record for this title is available from the British Library.

Get the most from this book

Everyone has to decide his or her own revision strategy, but it is essential to review your work, learn it and test your understanding. These Revision Notes will help you to do that in a planned way, topic by topic. Use this book as the cornerstone of your revision and don't hesitate to write in it — personalise your notes and check your progress by ticking off each section as you revise.

Tick to track your progress

Use the revision planner on pages iv–viii to plan your revision, topic by topic. Tick each box when you have:

● revised and understood a topic
● tested yourself
● practised the Now test yourself questions and gone online to check your answers

You can also keep track of your revision by ticking off each topic heading in the book. You may find it helpful to add your own notes as you work through each topic.

Features to help you succeed

Exam tips

Expert tips are given throughout the book to help you polish your exam technique in order to maximise your chances in the exam.

Now test yourself

These short, knowledge-based questions provide the first step in testing your learning. Answers are online.

Definitions and key words

Key words from the specification are highlighted in bold throughout the book and defined in the glossary.

Revision activities

These activities will help you to understand each topic in an interactive way.

Diagrams

There are several diagrams throughout the book to aid understanding. We encourage you to draw diagrams that establish the connections between ideas and arguments as part of your revision.

Exam checklist

A checklist to tick off to keep track of the things you need to know for each part of the exam.

Key quotes

Quotations from philosophers about a specific topic.

Criticism

Highlights and evaluates some of the difficulties in various ideas.

Online

Go online to check your answers to the Now test yourself questions at **www.hoddereducation. co.uk/myrevisionnotesdownloads**

My revision planner

REVISED   TESTED   EXAM READY

REVISED   TESTED   EXAM READY

Section 2 Moral philosophy

Normative theories

REVISED   TESTED   EXAM READY

Countdown to my exams

6–8 weeks to go

- Start by looking at the specification — make sure you know exactly what material you need to revise and the style of the examination. Use the revision planner on pages iv–viii to familiarise yourself with the topics.
- Organise your notes, making sure you have covered everything on the specification. The revision planner will help you to group your notes into topics.
- Work out a realistic revision plan that will allow you time for relaxation. Set aside days and times for all the subjects that you need to study, and stick to your timetable.
- Set yourself sensible targets. Break your revision down into focused sessions of around 40 minutes, divided by breaks. These Revision Notes organise the basic facts into short, memorable sections to make revising easier.

REVISED ☐

2–6 weeks to go

- Read through the relevant sections of this book and refer to the exam tips, exam checklists and key terms. Tick off the topics as you feel confident about them. Highlight those topics you find difficult and look at them again in detail.
- Test your understanding of each topic by working through the 'Now test yourself' questions in the book. Look up the answers online.
- Make a note of any problem areas as you revise, and ask your teacher to go over these in class.
- Look at past papers. They are one of the best ways to revise and practise your exam skills.
- Use the revision activities to try out different revision methods. For example, you can make notes using mind maps, spider diagrams or flash cards.
- Track your progress using the revision planner and give yourself a reward when you have achieved your target.

REVISED ☐

One week to go

- Try to fit in at least one more timed practice of an entire past paper and seek feedback from your teacher, comparing your work closely with the mark scheme.
- Check the revision planner to make sure you haven't missed out any topics. Brush up on any areas of difficulty by talking them over with a friend or getting help from your teacher.
- Attend any revision classes put on by your teacher. Remember, he or she is an expert at preparing people for examinations.

REVISED ☐

The day before the examination

- Flick through these Revision Notes for useful reminders, for example the exam tips, exam checklists and key terms.
- Check the time and place of your examination.
- Make sure you have everything you need — extra pens and pencils, tissues, a watch, bottled water, sweets.
- Allow some time to relax and have an early night to ensure you are fresh and alert for the examinations.

REVISED ☐

My exam

Paper 1: Epistemology and moral philosophy

Date:...

Time: ....

Location: ....

Exam support

The Assessment Objectives

The AQA A-level Philosophy specification has two Assessment Objectives (AOs). These tell the examiners what they should look for in your answers.

AO1 concerns how well you are able to show your *understanding* of the topic, ideas, methods and arguments and your ability to analyse and explain them by identifying the key ideas and showing how they fit together.

AO2 tests your capacity to *analyse* philosophical positions, theories and arguments in order that you may *evaluate* how strong they are by exploring the quality of the reasoning, considering their implications and exploring objections and counter arguments.

The exam

The A-level exam consists of two, three-hour papers. Paper 1 examines *Epistemology* and *Moral philosophy*. Paper 2, the *Metaphysics of God* and *Metaphysics of Mind*. Both exam papers will contain 10 questions, 5 on **each** theme:

- 1 × 3-mark question (all 3 marks awarded for AO1)
- 2 × 5-mark questions (all 5 marks awarded for AO1)
- 1 × 12-mark question (all 12 marks awarded for AO1)
- 1 × 25-mark question (5 marks awarded for AO1, 20 marks for AO2)

The *only* time you can gain marks for showing your ability to analyse and evaluate (AO2) is in answering the 25-mark question. In the other question because marks are awarded for AO1 only, you will not be credited for evaluating the arguments.

Timings

In the exam, try to divide your time evenly between the two themes (1.5 hours on each). Practise answering questions under timed conditions to get a feel for the amount you can write in the time. These are rough guidelines

- 3-mark question: 3–5 minutes
- 5-mark questions: 5–10 minutes (× 2)
- 12-mark question: 15–25 minutes
- 25-mark question: 40–50 minutes

The questions

Exams are not really the time for *new* or *experimental* thinking. They are about drawing selectively on what you have learnt and framing it in a way that communicates effectively in response to the precise question.

Read a question carefully and make sure you are clear about its focus. Organise your material clearly and coherently. In the longer questions, this means briefly planning the order in which you will present the ideas and including a conclusion and an introduction (see below). In the shorter answer questions, this means answering the questions concisely but precisely.

Three-mark questions

These test your grasp of essential concepts that you have covered on the course and your ability to encapsulate them with precision. They may ask you to provide a definition, or briefly outline an idea or theory.

- As a rough rule, try to answer in just one or two sentences.
- Think carefully about the wording, try to be economical and precise.
- Examples are usually not needed, and if used should be kept brief.

Practice questions

Epistemology (3 marks)	Moral philosophy (3 marks)
1 What is a tautology?	1 What is meant by 'maximising utility'?
2 What is abduction?	2 What is the first formulation of the categorical imperative?
3 What is indirect realism?	3 What is eudaimonia?
4 What is solipsism?	4 What is a dilemma?
5 What is a contingent truth?	5 What, is moral nihilism?

Five-mark questions

These questions will usually ask you to outline or explain an idea, theory or argument issue.

- Again, try to be as clear and precise as possible.
- Explain the different elements of the idea and how they are connected.

- When focusing on arguments, try to show how the argument might be structured. Be clear about the distinction between the premises and conclusion of an argument or the connections between the elements of a theory.
- You may include illustrative examples to support your account, which could be drawn from the texts, but only if relevant.

Practice questions

Epistemology (5 marks)	Ethics (5 marks)
1 Explain a Gettier counter example to the tripartite definition of knowledge.	1 What is the naturalistic fallacy?
2 Explain the argument that indirect realism leads to scepticism about the external world.	2 Explain the difference between act and rule utilitarianism.
3 Explain one argument for drawing the primary/secondary quality distinction.	3 Outline Aristotle's function argument.
4 Explain Berkeley's Master Argument.	4 Explain the difference between cognitivism and non-cognitivism.
5 Explain Leibniz's argument for innatism based on necessary truths.	5 Explain Mackie's 'error theory'.

Twelve-mark questions (AO1)

These will ask you to explain a more substantial aspect of the syllabus. Perhaps a theory *and* an objection or to explain how a theory may be applied.

- As your answer will be longer try to organise the material so that it is not just accurate, but is structured into a coherent whole.
- Identify the key elements of the theory or argument and try to show how it fits together into a logical structure which makes sense. It may be helpful to illustrate your answers with examples either drawn from the texts or some of your own.
- You should not evaluate the argument/theory as no marks are available for AO2 (analysis and evaluation)

Practice questions

Epistemology (12 marks)	Moral philosophy (12 marks)
1 Explain how virtue epistemology seeks to define knowledge.	1 Explain how a utilitarian might condemn simulated killings in video games.
2 Explain why Locke rejects the doctrine of innate ideas.	2 Explain the tyranny of the majority objection to utilitarianism and how utilitarianism might be defended.
3 Explain Russell's response to scepticism about the existence of mind-independent objects.	3 Explain Aristotle's doctrine of the mean and how it applies to a particular virtue.
4 Explain how Berkeley tries to overcome scepticism about the external world.	4 Explain Philippa Foot's claim that morality is a system of hypothetical rather than categorical imperatives.
5 Outline Descartes' ontological argument for the existence of God and explain one objection to it.	5 Explain G.E. Moore's attack on naturalism in his Open Question Argument and the view this leads him to adopt (intuitionism).

Twenty-five-mark questions (5 AO1 + 20 AO2)

The 25-mark questions involve not just outlining a philosophical theory or view, but engaging meaningfully with the arguments for yourself and trying to defend a point of view. These are the only questions that test your capacity to develop an argument in defence of your own judgement.

- Introduce your answer by briefly outlining what the question is asking and unpack the issues raised in the question.
- Analyse the relevant arguments and concepts. Then work through a series of arguments.
- When selecting points for discussion, make sure they are directly relevant to the question and also explain why they are relevant.
- When exploring the arguments, try to avoid merely juxtaposing different philosophers' views on the topic. Instead, examine the cogency of

each view by looking at the reasons that support it and making a judgement about how strong the support is. Say something about whether you are rejecting or supporting the position.

- If you can make each point, follow from the previous point, this will help to give the essay a sense of overall development, which is something examiners will be looking for when awarding AO2 marks.
- Develop a coherent overall argument in support of a judgement. A conclusion is **not** a summary; it should be a *judgement* which responds to the question.
- Some questions will use key terms such as 'assess', 'critically discuss' and 'evaluate'. Other questions contain a less obvious request to evaluate *(Is it wrong to eat animals?)* but the basic task, as outlined above, will be the same.

Revision

- A good start is to break down the A-level syllabus into chunks. (This book is arranged into suitable chunks.)
- For each chunk it may be useful to go through your notes and textbooks with the aim of producing a few sides of revision notes (particularly of those elements you find hard to remember).
- Repeat this process, reducing your notes further (perhaps to cards).
- Some students like to make revision timetables outlining which days/evenings they will spend on which chunks.
- Start as early as you can. Now is always a good time!

Practice questions: 25 marks

Epistemology (25 marks)	Ethics (25 marks)
1 Is the world as it appears?	1 Is happiness the only good?
2 Are all concepts derived from experience?	2 Are the consequences of actions relevant to moral decisions?
3 Can knowledge be defined?	3 Is eating meat morally justifiable?
4 Is knowledge possible?	4 Does virtue ethics provide useful guidance on how to live?
5 Assess the view that all that exists are minds and their ideas (idealism).	5 Are all moral judgements false?

Section 1 Epistemology

Introduction

Epistemology is the area of philosophy that explores the nature of **knowledge**. This encompasses the key areas of: *what knowledge is, where it might come from* (**reason**, **perception**) and *whether it is even possible in the first place* (the limits of knowledge).

What is knowledge?

Types of knowledge

Philosophers have traditionally divided knowledge into three main types:
- practical knowledge (knowing 'how')
- knowledge by acquaintance (knowing 'of')
- propositional knowledge (knowing 'that').

Three kinds of knowledge

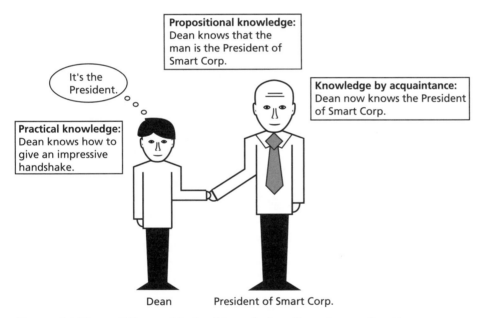

Propositional knowledge: Dean knows that the man is the President of Smart Corp.

It's the President.

Knowledge by acquaintance: Dean now knows the President of Smart Corp.

Practical knowledge: Dean knows how to give an impressive handshake.

Dean   President of Smart Corp.

Figure 1.1 Three different kinds of knowledge. Dean is meeting the president of Smart Corp.

The three forms of knowledge all come into play.

Propositional knowledge and language

Factual/propositional knowledge can always be expressed in language (not necessarily the case for the other two types):
- A proposition is a sentence that makes a claim about the world such as 'I am hungry' or 'There are four fish in the bowl'.
- What is asserted by such sentences is called a proposition, and for this reason factual knowledge is often called propositional knowledge.

The section on the definition of knowledge is primarily concerned with factual, propositional knowledge.

The nature of definition

Defining knowledge would help us understand what it is. But there are different types of definition. Linda Zagzebski argues that these definitions depend on the different natures of the **concepts** or objects involved.

- Some objects have what Locke called a real essence (a real, underlying cause that makes a thing the way it is). For example, water has a real essence, it is the way it is because of its chemical composition H_2O. If an object has a real essence, then it can have a real definition.
- In contrast, consider 'weeds'. There is no underlying cause that makes weeds weeds. There is no genetic difference between weeds and non-weeds. The classification is culturally specific – a question of which plants humans like in their gardens. We can still give a definition for the term 'weed', but it will not be a real definition, as weeds do not have a real essence.

Can knowledge have a real definition?

Zagzebski is sceptical about whether knowledge has a real essence. The term has varied so much in its use historically, which suggests the concept may be a socially constructed one. However, she recommends we treat knowledge as if it does have a real essence, so should seek a real definition. We should only give up if we are defeated in the project.

The role of cause in definition

Definitions also differ in the role that 'causes' play. Some emphasise the cause of the thing being defined, others do not. For example, a definition of sunburn would not just outline the symptoms, but also what *caused* the sunburn (UV light). In contrast, in defining a bicycle, there would be no mention of how bicycles were made/caused.

Pitfalls to avoid

Zagzebski outlines some pitfalls to avoid in giving any sort of definition. Definitions should **not** be:

- *Circular.* This means they should not include the term being defined – for example, saying that *justice* is what happens when *just* acts occur.
- *Obscure.* The terms in any definition should not be more obscure than the original term.
- *Negative.* Defining a term by what it is not does not help. For example, defining a good act as 'one that is not wrong'.
- *Ad hoc.* This means coming up with a definition that is specific to meeting a particular problem – for example, defining knowledge as *a justified true belief that is not a Gettier counter-example.*

> **Revision activity**
>
> Creating mnemonics can help to lodge some parts of the specification into your memory. For example, looking at the list of pitfalls in providing definitions, it might be more helpful to imagine that Zagzebski has labelled some definitions **A CON**. That is, **A**d Hoc, **C**ircular, **O**bscure and **N**egative. Try creating mnemonics for bits of the specification that you find harder to recall.

The tripartite view

In his dialogue, the *Meno*, Plato tries to work out the difference between someone having a true **belief** and someone having knowledge.

- Imagine travelling to a town (Plato's example is Larissa) with a guide who *knows* the way. In this case the guide would be a good one.
- But equally if you were travelling with a guide who merely guessed the way correctly, then she too would be a good guide.
- In both cases you end up in the right town. If my beliefs are true, then they are just as useful to me as 'knowledge'. So why should we prefer knowledge over true belief?

Now test yourself answers at **www.hoddereducation.co.uk/myrevisionnotesdownloads**

In the *Meno*, Plato's answer has many facets, one aspect is the stability of knowledge compared with the flightiness of belief. He writes:

> True beliefs are a fine thing and do all sorts of good so long as they stay in their place; but they will not stay long. They run away from a man's mind, so they are not worth much until you tether them by working out the reason ... Once they are tied down, they become knowledge, and are stable. That is why knowledge is something more valuable than right belief. What distinguishes one from the other is the tether.
>
> Plato, *Meno*, Penguin (1956) 97a–b (translation modified)

- Plato is saying that part of the reason we value knowledge is that it is more steadfast than mere belief, since it is backed up by reasons or **evidence**.
- The evidence acts as a kind of glue, which retains the belief in the mind by giving us good reason to continue believing it. By contrast, a belief for which we have no evidence – even if it happens to be true – has nothing to make it stick in the mind. So, to have knowledge is to have a true belief secured by reasons.
- In the *Theaetetus*, Plato offers similar considerations in support of this idea. He suggests that sometimes a jury might find a man guilty correctly, but for poor reasons (perhaps guessing). We would not want to say that the jury *knew* the man was guilty. So not every case of true belief is a case of knowledge.
- Plato's point is that we can hold true beliefs that we would be reluctant to call knowledge because of the nature of the evidence supporting them.
- In the *Theaetetus* Plato suggests that 'true belief accompanied by a rational account is knowledge', or, as we might say, knowledge is a *justified, true belief.*

Necessary and sufficient conditions

- A **necessary condition** is something you need in order to have the thing in question. Water is a necessary condition of rain. You cannot have rain without water. But water alone is not enough to guarantee rain. A lake does not count as rain. Water is a necessary but not **sufficient condition** of rain.
- Sufficient conditions, when met, mean that you will always have the thing in question. Being an aunt is a sufficient condition for having relatives. "Aunthood" guarantees relatives, but is it not a necessary condition, as a person can have relatives without being an aunt.
- Some conditions are both necessary and jointly (when put together) sufficient. Having never been married and being a man are the necessary and jointly sufficient conditions for being a bachelor. Being a man that has never been married makes you a bachelor (jointly sufficient) and you cannot be a bachelor without these two conditions being met (they are both necessary).
- The justified true belief definition of knowledge is saying that belief, truth and justification are the individually necessary and jointly sufficient conditions for knowledge.

Issues with the tripartite view

Issue: are the JTB conditions individually necessary?

The belief condition (B): can you have knowledge without belief?

The belief condition says that a necessary condition for your knowing that p is that you *believe* that p. Indeed, it would seem to be incoherent to say, 'I know that it is raining, but I do not believe it'.

- Some dispute that belief is a necessary condition of knowledge (so it is possible to know that p, but not believe that p). The apparent incoherence of saying 'I know it is raining, but I don't believe it' stems from the fact that belief is a necessary condition to honestly assert anything. So no-one would assert that it is raining, without believing it. But beyond asserting, belief may not be needed for knowledge.
- Some equate knowledge more with successful action. For example, you might hesitantly get the answer correct to a quiz question (having been taught it correctly, but do not remember being taught). In this case some would argue that you knew it, even though you did not really believe it.
- Some have claimed that knowledge and belief are very different sorts of mental states. In the *Meno* and *Theaetetus* Plato argued that knowledge entails belief, but in a later work, *The Republic*, he claimed they are separate. He reasoned that since knowledge is infallible and belief is fallible, they must be fundamentally different ways of apprehending the world. Knowledge involves going *beyond* mere belief.

The truth condition (T): can you have knowledge without truth?

Does a **fact** need to be true for you to know it? Often, we *claim* to know something that turns out to be false, but this does not mean that we actually do know it.

Imagine it is 10,000BC. Raquel, a cavewoman, believes the world is flat, based on the evidence available at the time. Is it possible that she *knew* the Earth was flat? The answer to this depends on how we define truth.

Correspondence theory of truth	Coherence theory of truth
This theory says that truth consists in a correspondence between a claim and the relevant fact. In this theory the claim (the world is flat) does not correspond to the fact, so it is not true. Raquel cannot know the world is flat as her (somewhat) justified belief is not *true*.	The coherence theory of truth has different varieties, but one kind proposes that a belief is true if it is one of the web of beliefs held by a society to be true. This web of beliefs is internally coherent, with the beliefs supporting one another. So back in Raquel's day, the web of true beliefs would have included the claim that the world was flat. On the coherence theory, Raquel did have a justified, true belief and did know the world was flat.

Although these theories of truth differ, you can still argue that truth is one of the conditions of knowledge. It is just that using the coherence theory of truth, we are more inclined to allow people to have 'known' things in the past – things that we no longer would count as knowledge now. And this is because the concept of truth was bound to the belief system of that time, not of our time.

In contrast, the correspondence theory claims that the facts do not change over time. So, it was never true that the world was flat and Raquel never knew it was. However, both theories require knowledge to be true.

The evidence/justification condition (J): can you have knowledge without justification?

Imagine a friend guesses that a dice will land on six. It does. We are reluctant to say she knew this, as true belief alone is not enough – a valid justification is needed (for example, it was a loaded dice).

But some disagree about the justification element. **Reliabilism** (see **page 9**) claims that knowledge is a true belief that has been reliably generated – a conscious 'justification' may not be necessary. Consider this scenario:

> John has a rare gift. If you give him any date in the future, say 15 March 2123, he is able to tell you what day of the week this will be (for example, a Monday). He is unable to say how he does this, though he is incredibly accurate.

Would you say that John *knows* what day it will be on 15 March 2123? This is a case of true belief, but with no rational justification. How John gets the answers right is a mystery, but he *is* very reliable. Justification may not always be necessary for knowledge.

Issue: are the JTB conditions jointly sufficient?

REVISED

Each condition may be individually necessary for knowledge, but are they jointly sufficient? If you have all three, are you guaranteed to have knowledge? Does J + T + B = K?

Cases of lucky true belief: Gettier counter-examples

One way of showing that the JTB conditions are *not* sufficient is to give examples of JTBs that do not count as knowledge. One philosopher, Edmund Gettier did just this. Gettier published a short paper entitled 'Is justified, true belief knowledge?' The paper was only three pages long, but had a large impact.

Gettier's first example – the job

Smith and Jones are both going for a job. Smith has strong evidence that his rival Jones will get the job (the president of the company told him so). Smith also has strong evidence that Jones has ten coins in his pocket (he counted them). Smith forms the belief that *the man who will get the job has ten coins in his pocket*. As it turns out, Smith (not Jones) gets the job. Also, by coincidence, Smith has exactly ten coins in his pocket. So, Smith's belief that *the man who will get the job has ten coins in his pocket* was a) a belief, b) true, c) justified (to some extent).

But most people would claim that Smith did *not* have knowledge, because luck was involved. He was unlucky that his belief about Jones getting the job was wrong, and was lucky that he also happened to have ten coins in his pocket.

It seems we have an anti-luck intuition. We do not want to award knowledge on the basis of luck.

Smith has evidence that his friend Jones owns a Ford (imagine he saw Jones driving it that day). Smith believes that *Jones owns a Ford*. Smith has another friend Brown. He has no evidence of Mr Brown's whereabouts, but on the strength of his first belief forms a new disjunctive belief (joining two different beliefs) that *Jones owns a Ford OR Brown is in Barcelona* (Barcelona is chosen at random). This new belief is justified as Smith had no reason to doubt the first part.

It turns out that Jones no longer owns a car (perhaps he sold it last week and has been driving a hire car) but by a weird coincidence, Brown, unbeknown to Smith, was in Barcelona. His belief that *Jones owns a Ford OR Brown is in Barcelona* was true and was justified – but did he know it? Most of us would say not, as again there seems to be luck involved.

Revision activity

Practise writing out one of Gettier's examples. Can you clearly articulate how it shows that the three conditions for knowledge (JTB) are individually met, but that they are not jointly sufficient for knowledge?

Double-luck Gettiers are inevitable on JTB account

Zagzebski argues that the JTB account of knowledge will always leave a gap between the justification and the truth (only **infallibilism** says that justification must guarantee the truth).

Because of this gap we can always generate Gettier-style cases that rely on double luck (the justification being unluckily wrong, the belief being luckily true).

- She gives an example of a doctor who believes *a patient has virus X*. The tests show this is the only virus consistent with the evidence (strong inductive evidence).
- However, the symptoms are actually caused by a new, unknown virus Y (she was unlucky with her prior justification).
- But, it turns out, the patient does have virus X too, but at a stage that is too early to show up in tests (so her belief was luckily true).
- This is a standard-type Gettier counter-example and most would say that, because of the luck involved, the doctor did not know the patient had virus X.

Zagzebski claims that only by linking the justification to the truth of the belief can we avoid Gettier-style cases like these. Only when true beliefs are held *because* of the justification should we claim knowledge (this is the approach **virtue epistemology** takes).

Fake barns

As well as the double-luck Gettiers there is another type of counter-example to the JTB account of knowledge. This type also relies on luck, but in a different way. Consider this scenario:

Barney is driving, unknowingly, through a place called fake-barn county –lots of fake barns have been built consisting of just a barn front with nothing behind (like on a movie set). Barney looks to the side and sees a big red barn. On the basis of this he believes there is a big red barn by the road. However, it just so happens that this is the only real barn in the whole area! Does Barney know there was a big red barn there?

In the fake barn case, Barney saw a real barn with his eyes, believed there was a real barn and there was a real barn. The luck involved is that it happened to be the only real barn for miles and he had no idea that the others were fakes. This relies on the wider context making the belief seem luckily true. So, we can define the two types as:

● Gettier counter-examples. These involve a double luck. The justification unluckily not applying but the belief luckily being true anyway.
● Fake barn cases. The justification is not false in any way, but the believer does not know that she is in an unusual context which makes her belief seem luckily true.

If these examples of JTBs do not count as knowledge, then it seems that JTB cannot be the sufficient conditions for knowledge.

Responses to the issues with the tripartite view

Infallibilism

REVISED

Gettier-style counter-examples rely on cases where there is luck involved. One way to remove this element of luck from the process is to require the justification to be so strong that the truth is guaranteed – in other words, to claim that knowledge can only be allowed if the belief is infallible (meaning impossible to be wrong).

● Infallibilism is *not* the claim that we must *feel* certain in our beliefs to have knowledge. Certainty is a subjective feeling that can fluctuate with moods.
● Infallibilism is the theory that we should only count as knowledge those things which we cannot rationally doubt. For example, you cannot rationally doubt that you exist, that you are now seeing black marks on a white background and that $2 + 2 = 4$.

Infallibilism and Gettier

Infallibilism is not open to Gettier or fake barn cases as none of these examples would count as knowledge. All the counter-examples are open to some doubt/alternative explanations so cannot be claimed as 'knowledge'. Once knowledge is restricted to those things that cannot be doubted, there is no room for Gettier counter-examples to thrive.

Infallibilism: knowledge and belief

Some infallibilists argue we should distinguish belief from knowledge. They claim that knowledge is not a kind of belief, but a separate thing. Beliefs only occur when doubt *is* possible and knowledge occurs when it is impossible.

● To show this difference, the philosopher Price cites the example of pain. When you are in pain, you *know* you are; you cannot be wrong.
● He claims that it makes no sense to say you *also* believe you are in pain, as you know you are. It is just not an issue of belief.
● Someone else may observe you and infer that you are in pain. In this case, the person would hold a *belief* about your pain. They would not know you were in pain – as there is the possibility of an alternative explanation/error (you could be faking it!).
● But there is no possibility of your being wrong about your pain, so you *know* that you are in pain.

Criticism

The main criticism of infallibilism is that it goes against our **intuition** that we can know lots of things. Infallibilism would imply that we have very little knowledge – perhaps some logical truths and some facts about our minds, such as the **sensations** we experience. But most of our claims about the world, history, science and so on, would only be classed as beliefs.

Most philosophers are reluctant to pursue such a radical redefinition of our ordinary view of what counts as knowledge. To diverge too radically from common usage involves leaving behind the very concept we are setting out to define. Only by holding some sort of connection with ordinary usage can we be said to be analysing the concept of knowledge at all.

On the positive side, infallibilism is not open to Gettier counter-examples. Another positive feature of this theory is that it accords with our intuition that knowledge involves a level of certainty – although in this case it is absolute certainty.

No false lemmas: J + T + B + N

REVISED

A **lemma** is a premise accepted as true in an argument.

The no false lemma account argues that in Gettier's two scenarios, because the 'justification' includes a false belief or lemma, they should not be considered as examples of knowledge.

In the first case, Smith's belief that *the man who will get the job has ten coins in his pocket* (see **page 5**) was based on the false belief that Jones would get the job. Smith's reasoning might resemble this:

P1 I believe that Jones has ten coins in his pocket (having seen them).

P2 I believe that Jones will get the job (having been told as much).

C I believe that the person who gets the job will have ten coins in his pocket.

However, P2 is a false belief. It is a false lemma.

Gettier's second example also involves the use of a false belief in the believer's reasoning (that Jones owns a Ford).

To eliminate these counter-examples, the no false lemma theory claims that knowledge is a justified, true belief, where the justification is not based on a false belief. To put it more formally, it claims that: knowledge = J + T + B + N (where N = no false lemmas).

This theory adds an extra 'external' element to the account of the knowledge –that beliefs or assumptions used in the justification must be true.

On some levels the theory seems reasonable. In most cases, when we justify a belief using a false lemma, the belief itself will turn out to be false.

● For example, if you were checking the football results, without realising the newspaper was a year old, most of your beliefs about the scores would be false.

● However, if one result happened to be true by coincidence, then we would not want to count this as knowledge, as we do not want knowledge to be based on false beliefs (in this case that the paper was today's).

> **Exam tip**
>
> Three-mark questions often ask you to explain a particular term or idea. Can you clearly and briefly explain what a false lemma is?

Criticism

The theory copes well with Gettier's two cases. However, in other cases it is not so clear that a false belief was involved. Take the example from Zagzebski above (**page 6**). The doctor bases her diagnosis on the inductive evidence that everyone with those symptoms and test results has virus X. Based on this she concludes the patient has virus X. But there is no false belief used in this justification.

Additionally, for the fake barn case, Barney sees a barn and forms the belief that it is a barn. So there is no false belief. You could argue there are hidden background assumptions based in both cases (that only virus X causes the symptoms, and assuming that the surroundings were normal rather than fake), but not false beliefs.

Reliabilism: R + T + B

REVISED

Reliabilism has many variations, all based around a simple idea, which is to link knowledge with the reliability of the process that led to it.

● Consider the difference between quality newspapers and gossip columns. We trust one more than the other precisely because one is a more reliable source of information, meaning that it produces the truth more often. Reliability is defined in terms of truth giving.

● Likewise, with your beliefs. We should only grant the status of knowledge to those beliefs that have been formed by reliable cognitive processes – processes that are highly likely to result in true belief – such as seeing things up close, simple arithmetic and reading from a trustworthy source.

● Cognitive processes such as wishfully believing, complex mental arithmetic and guessing do not regularly produce true beliefs and so are not reliable. The beliefs they generate should not be classed as knowledge.

Replacing 'justified' with 'reliably formed'

Reliabilism suggests that knowledge is a true belief formed by a reliable process. The reliable process *replaces* the justified condition.

This is quite a change. Justifications are *internal* to the believer, they involve conscious thoughts: 'I saw it with my own eyes'. However, a reliable cognitive process does not necessarily involve conscious thoughts (though most of the time it will). Consider John, the calendar man (see **page 5**). Using the JTB definition, John would **not** know what day of the week it would be as he lacks a proper conscious justification for his belief. According to reliabilism, John does know what the date will be. His accuracy means the process is reliable.

Advantages of replacing J with R

Animals

Reliabilism can provide an account of how animals have knowledge. Using the JTB account, animals are unlikely to have knowledge as they cannot justify their beliefs. In contrast, a reliabilist might claim that animals have evolved to have reliable processes of vision, cognition, memory etc. These reliable processes mean they can interact successfully with the world and so we can say they have knowledge about it.

Cognitive science

Defining knowledge in terms of reliable processes may help move the whole issue from philosophy into cognitive science. Instead of philosophers giving 'internal' accounts of which justifications are good ones, cognitive scientists can give 'external' accounts of the neurological processes that lead to true belief.

Criticism

One criticism of reliabilism is how it accounts for brain in a vat scenarios (BIV). Hold up your pen. Do you believe it is there? In the JTB account your belief in the pen is justified in both BIV and normal worlds (the evidence is the same). But in the BIV world, it is not true. This seems right. If the experience is exactly the same, then the belief is justified in both worlds.

Reliabilism differs. In the normal world your pen belief is produced by a reliable process (holding and seeing produces true belief). But in the BIV world the belief is not produced by a reliable process (does not produce truth) – even though the experience and cognitive processes are identical. But, given the experience is the same, don't we want to say that the belief is equally justified in both worlds? The criticism is that in replacing the concept of 'justification' with 'reliably produced', reliabilism does not give an adequate account of the relationship between our beliefs and our justifications.

Reliabilism and Gettier: the problem

Most counter-examples are based on the initial belief being caused by fairly reliable processes (Barney sees a barn). The belief, whether justified or reliably produced, then turns out to be 'luckily' true. In this way the RTB account fares no better than the standard JTB account of knowledge in being 'Gettiered'. But, just as philosophers have tried to 'patch up' the JTB account, similar approaches have been tried with the RTB account.

Patching up reliabilism 1: redefining the process

Knowledge is true belief resulting from a reliable process. But how a process is described can make a difference to how reliable we deem it. The second Gettier example could be described as a case of inferring from a *false belief* (that *Jones owns a Ford*) to a new belief. Inferring from a false belief is not a reliable process (as the no false lemmas theory suggests).

In the case of the fake barn, seeing an object close up is usually a reliable way of forming true beliefs. However, the process could be redescribed as a case of *visual identification in highly deceptive circumstances* (fake barn county) – which, of course, is not reliable.

This approach solves many cases but does raise a general concern about how general or specific we should be when describing a belief-forming process.

Patching up reliabilism 2: no relevant alternatives

Goldman suggests we should only count a process as reliable if it can distinguish between the truth and other relevant possibilities.

Imagine you know identical twins: Trudy and Judy. You bump into one, and believe it is Judy. It is. Would you be able to tell if in fact it was Trudy?

Now test yourself answers at **www.hoddereducation.co.uk/myrevisionnotesdownloads**

If not, then your process of identifying the twin is not reliable enough, as it could not distinguish between the truth (Judy) and a relevant alternative (Trudy). As such, you would not *know* it was Judy. However, if you *can* reliably tell them apart, then you would know it was Judy.

This approach deals well with many counter-examples. In fake barn county, is Barney able to distinguish between seeing a real barn and seeing a relevant alternative (in this case, a fake barn)? Probably not. In which case, his belief was not formed from a reliable process and Barney did not know there was a barn there.

Virtue epistemology: V + T + B

Virtue epistemology seeks to justify knowledge in terms of the intellectual virtues and vices of the knower.
- In virtue ethics, an act of kindness would be one that achieves its goal (giving a present to a friend) and that sprang from the virtue of kindness.
- A virtuous act is successful and its success stems from virtue.
- Likewise, with intellectual acts, an act of knowledge occurs when the belief is successful (it is true) and where its success *stems* from intellectual virtue (so is not just luckily true).

Intellectual virtues

Reliabilism claims that some processes such as *remembering recent events* and *reasoning well* usually lead to true beliefs, whereas others such as *reading astrology charts* do not. The tendency (often called the disposition) to use reliable processes is an intellectual virtue. The tendency to use unreliable processes is an intellectual vice. Virtue epistemology claims that knowledge is a true belief brought about by a virtuous intellectual disposition – in other words, a virtuous true belief.

Triple A rating ('AAA')

Sosa compares cases of knowing with athletic performances including archery. In accurately shooting an arrow, Sosa identifies three key elements:
1 *Accuracy* – whether it hits the target. An accurate shot hits the target (even if luckily so). Likewise, a belief is accurate if it is true.
2 *Adroitness* – how skilful it was. An adroit shot is skilful – even if it misses (perhaps because of a gust of wind). Likewise, an *adroit* belief is one formed by an intellectual virtue (even if not true).
3 *Aptness* – an apt shot is one that is accurate *because* it was adroit (skilful). An *apt* belief is one that is true *because* it was formed with intellectual virtue.

Knowledge as apt belief

Sosa suggests knowledge is **apt belief**. This third element, aptness, is key. Both Gettier cases involved an accurate belief (*the successful candidate has ten coins*). The beliefs were fairly adroit (skilful) (counting the coins, being tipped off by the president). However, the trueness of the belief was not a result of any intellectual virtue; it was just coincidence. It was an accurate, skilful belief, but crucially it was not apt – not accurate *because* of the skill (intellectual virtue). Under Sosa's version of virtue epistemology, Smith's beliefs would not count as knowledge.

Now test yourself

Explain how accuracy, adroitness and aptness relate to the performance of shooting an arrow and also (with examples) to the performance of forming a belief.

TESTED

Fake barns

Barney's belief about the barn would seem to have an AAA rating. It was accurate (there was a barn), adroit (based on visual perception) and apt (accurate because it was adroit). So, it should be a case of knowledge. Yet many would not count this as knowledge.

Animal and human (reflective) knowledge

Sosa suggests that Barney *does* have a form of knowledge, which he termed *animal* knowledge – the sort that other animals have too.

To have *human* knowledge also requires the believer to have an awareness about how apt, or otherwise, their belief is. Human knowledge requires the ability to reflect on your belief. Consider archery again:

● On an incredibly windy day, a skilful archer shoots and hits the bull's-eye.
● The shot was apt – it hit the target because of the skill of the archer.
● However, the archer knew that hitting the target on such a windy day might take twenty shots, so a strong element of luck was involved.
● The shot was apt, but in this case the archer can reflect and form a belief about how lucky, or not, the shot was.

Contrast this with Barney who is unaware he is in fake barn county. Barney has animal knowledge (his belief is apt), but he does *not* have reflective (human) knowledge. He cannot tell if his belief is apt or not, nor make a judgement about whether it was lucky or not. If Barney was aware of his unusual context, he would then be able to form a reflective belief about the likely accuracy of his initial belief. Indeed, Barney may not even claim to know there was a barn.

> **Revision activity**
>
> Create a table with the four responses to Gettier: *infallibilism, no false lemmas, reliabilism* and *virtue epistemology*. For each theory, state how it defines knowledge. Then briefly say how it copes/fails to cope with: a) standard Gettier cases, b) fake barn-style cases. Also state any strengths and weaknesses.

Exam checklist

You should be able to:	✓
Give definitions and examples of *ability knowledge (know how)*	
Give definitions and examples of *acquaintance knowledge*	
Give definitions and examples of *propositional knowledge*	
Discuss different types of definition and pitfalls to be avoided	
Outline why knowledge might be defined as justified true belief – with reference to Plato	
Discuss whether justification is individually necessary for knowledge	
Discuss whether truth is individually necessary for knowledge	
Discuss whether belief is individually necessary for knowledge	
Evaluate whether the three conditions are *jointly sufficient*, with reference to the *two Gettier* examples and the *fake barn* example.	
Outline and evaluate (also discuss whether it overcomes the Gettier cases): *Infallibilism*	
Outline and evaluate (also discuss whether it overcomes the Gettier cases): *No false lemmas*	
Outline and evaluate (also discuss whether it overcomes the Gettier cases): *Reliabilism*	
Outline and evaluate (also discuss whether it overcomes the Gettier cases): *Epistemic virtue*	

Perception as a source of knowledge

Introduction

Both in science and in everyday life, we are interested in having reliable beliefs about the world around us. While rationalist and **empiricist** philosophers have disagreed on the precise role that perception plays in the acquisition of such beliefs, few have gone so far as to suggest that it has none at all. But how exactly does perception provide us with beliefs about physical reality? A good starting point for exploring possible answers to this question is common sense. The direct realist view reflects the essentials of a common-sense approach.

Direct realism (naïve realism)

What is direct realism?

REVISED

There are two elements in perception: the perceiver and object perceived.
- To say there are two elements in perception is to say that there is no third thing *mediating* between the person who perceives and the physical object they perceive.
- So **direct realism** rejects the indirect realist notion of '**sense data**'.

We immediately perceive physical objects.
- If there is nothing mediating between perceiver and perceived, then we perceive physical objects 'immediately' (without mediation).
- So when we perceive the world we are directly aware of the objects themselves (so, again, no sense data).

Physical objects are mind-independent.
- This is a realist view because it means that the objects exist outside of the mind.
- So if you cease to perceive an object (for example, because you close your eyes) it doesn't cease to exist.

Our senses detect properties of these objects (colours, shapes, etc.) which exist in the world.
- It is not just the objects that exist independently of the perceiver's mind, it is also the properties of the objects that are mind-independent.

And objects retain these properties when unperceived.
- When you leave an apple in a drawer and forget about it, it remains round, hard, crisp, red and retains its flavour and smell.
- When a tree falls over in a forest when there's no one there to hear it, it still makes a sound.

Figure 1.2 We immediately perceive mind-independent objects – our senses detect properties such as colours which exist in the world, and objects keep these properties when they are not perceived.

> ### Revision activity
>
> Use an example of your own to illustrate the main tenets of direct realism.

> ### Exam tip
>
> For the 25-mark questions in the exam you will need to evaluate the relative merits of philosophical theories. The top-band responses need to support their conclusions with a *balanced* discussion. So you need both to examine **arguments** and counter-arguments and explore both the strengths and the weaknesses of different positions.

Support for direct realism

- Direct realism is in tune with common sense. In the *Problems of Philosophy* Russell argues that we should accept the common-sense opinions and beliefs we are inclined to by instinct, unless they lead to inconsistency.
- It avoids **scepticism**: it gives us a clear account of how it is that we come to have knowledge of the world: we know about it because our senses provide immediate access to its true nature.
- It has explanatory power. For if it is true that I am directly aware of physical reality and its properties, this explains why I am able to execute a whole range of practical actions on a daily basis, such as finding food that I need to survive.
- It explains why I perceive what I do. I see the tree as green because the tree is green. My perception of the tree is regular and predictable precisely because there exists a real tree beyond my mind which causes my perception of it. I have no control over what I see when I open my eyes, because there really are mind-independent objects causing me to perceive.
- Direct realism also explains why we agree about what we perceive and is in tune with our sense that we occupy the same universe as everyone else. If you and I stand before an apple tree we can expect there to be a high degree of agreement about the shape, size, colours, smells and so forth.

Issues with direct realism

Issue: argument from illusion

- It is well-known that our senses are subject to illusions from time to time. In such cases, our senses distort the true nature of physical reality in some way, so that what we seem to perceive is not the same as what is actually out there in the world.
- For example, when looking at a straight straw half-immersed in a glass of water from a certain angle, it will appear broken or bent.
- In such a case we are directly aware of the bent-looking straw and cannot doubt that this is the way it appears to us.
- At the same time we can be pretty confident that the real straw is not itself broken or bent.
- If the way the world appears to us in such cases is not the way the world actually is, then we must conclude that the immediate objects of perception cannot be **material** objects. We are forced, in other words, to distinguish appearances from reality.
- Formally we can present the argument as follows.
  - **P1** When subject to an illusion an object appears to a perceiver to have a particular property (for example, a straw appears to be bent).
  - **P2** The perceiver is directly aware of this apparent property (for example, of a bent-looking straw).
  - **P3** But the object doesn't have this property in reality (for example, the real straw is not bent).
  - **C1** So what the perceiver is directly aware of (the bent straw) and what is real (the straight straw) are distinct.
  - **C2** So direct realism is false: we do not perceive physical objects directly.

Indirect realists then go on to claim that the immediate objects of perception are sense data and that it is by means of our awareness of these sense data that we come to know about physical objects.

Response to this issue

- The second **premise**, however, may misrepresent the situation. When I am subject to an illusion, the direct realist may claim, it is not the case that I am directly aware of anything distinct from the physical object.
- There is no *thing* – the appearance of the straw – of which I am immediately aware and which we should contrast with the real straw.
- Rather, we should say that I am directly aware of the real straw, but that it appears bent because of the circumstances (the light travelling through two different mediums).
- This appearing is not another thing mediating between me and the straw. It is just the manner of the straw's appearance.
- So direct realists don't have to suppose that objects have to appear exactly as they are. And if we accept that they can appear differently because of the way they relate to the perceiver then we don't have to posit things called 'sense data'.
- In sum, the indirect realists' mistake is to 'reify appearances', that is to suppose we must explain illusions by positing the existence of entities called 'appearances' or 'sense data' which are directly observed.

Issue: perceptual variation

REVISED

The perceptual variation argument begins with the observation that the appearance of physical objects can vary depending on the conditions under which they are perceived. Bertrand Russell's discussion of his table in Chapter 1 of his *Problems of Philosophy* is a key passage which presents examples of such variation.

Russell's table example

- Russell argues that because his table appears white when the light is reflected off it, and brown otherwise, and there is no basis for privileging one colour over the other, then the table cannot be said to have a particular colour.
- The apparent shape also varies depending on the angle from which the table is observed. Since the table itself doesn't change its shape, we must distinguish the real table from the one appearing in our minds.
- Russell concludes that 'The real table ... is not *immediately* known to us at all, but must be an **inference** from what is immediately known.'
- The argument may be summarised as follows:

  P1 Direct realism claims that the immediate objects of perception are material objects and their properties (such as colours, textures and shapes).

  P2 But when we perceive physical objects the appearance of their properties can vary.

  P3 The properties of the objects themselves don't vary.

  C So direct realism is false: the apparent properties are not the same as the real properties of physical objects.

Indirect realists, such as Russell, then conclude that:
- the immediate objects of perception are appearances or sense data
- we must infer the existence and the real properties of objects on the basis of direct acquaintance with the sense data
- so, we do not perceive the world directly.

> **Exam tip**
>
> Read Chapter 1 of Russell's *Problems of Philosophy* and the first part of Berkeley's *First Dialogue* to familiarise yourself with the examples of perceptual variation they use. Use these examples in exam responses to demonstrate knowledge of the anthology texts.

Berkeley's example

- In *First Dialogue* Bishop George Berkeley employs a series of examples of perceptual variation to develop a similar argument to Russell.
- One is the bowl of water example which he borrows from John Locke: if you place one hot hand and one cold hand into a bowl of lukewarm water the water will appear cold to one and hot to the other.
- Berkeley uses this and similar observations to reduce to absurdity the realist claim that the perceived qualities exist in matter as they are perceived.
- Berkeley's argument is as follows:

  P1 Direct realism claims material objects possess mind-independent properties (such as heat/cold, tastes, smells and colours) which we directly perceive.

  P2 But material objects are perceived to have incompatible properties (for example, cold and hot at the same time).

  P3 They cannot possess incompatible properties in reality (this is contradictory).

  C Therefore direct realism is false: material objects do not possess such properties.

Berkeley's **conclusion** is rather stronger than Russell's. Russell doesn't deny that objects have real properties, only that we don't perceive them directly as they are. Berkeley's conclusion is that the perceived qualities of objects are in the mind, rather than in the objects.

Response to this issue

- The perceptual variation argument attacks the assumption of direct realism – that we perceive the properties of objects as they really are. But the direct realist can give up this rather naïve assumption, without necessarily giving up direct realism. The direct realist can accept that objects may appear differently to perceivers and yet insist that they are nonetheless directly perceived.
- For example, water which *is* lukewarm can *appear* cold to a perceiver. This doesn't mean it isn't lukewarm or that it isn't directly perceived. Nor does it mean that there must be something, the appearance of cold, which *is* directly perceived and distinct from the water itself.
- For it is a property of lukewarm water that it will appear warm to a cold hand and cold to a warm hand. Similarly, a table can appear white or beige, while being brown. Or it can appear trapezoid when it is rectangular.
- We have agreed methods for determining the correct temperature of the water and the true colour of the table. We rarely find ourselves facing genuine disagreement in such cases. If in any doubt we ensure the lighting conditions are normal and move around the table to avoid any glare. In this way we can tell the real colour.
- Finally, we can explain why the colour appears as it does from different angles in terms of the way light reflects from its surface. We can also explain why the water feels warm or cool – because of the temperatures of our hands relative to that of the water.
- Similar explanations for other examples of perceptual variation can be developed using direct realist assumptions. Tastes and smells can appear differently because of differences in the state of the organs of sense. So there is no need to posit the existence of some third thing, the appearance, mediating between the perceiver and perceived.

Now test yourself answers at **www.hoddereducation.co.uk/myrevisionnotesdownloads**

Issue: argument from hallucination

- Hallucinations occur when a person perceives something which isn't actually there.
- Often the person is unable to distinguish their hallucination from a **veridical** (truthful, accurate) perception.
- However, if a hallucination and a veridical perception are subjectively indistinguishable, then the person must be aware of the same thing in both cases.
- Since what the person is aware of in a hallucination is in the mind, what they are aware of during veridical perception must also be in the mind.
- So, during veridical perception, what we directly perceive are sense data in the mind, and we perceive the material world only indirectly.
- This argument can be summarised as:
  - **P1** Hallucinations occur when a person perceives something which doesn't exist outside the mind.
  - **C1** So what they perceive, the hallucination, exists only in their mind.
  - **P2** Hallucinations can be subjectively indistinguishable from veridical perceptions.
  - **P3** But if hallucinations and veridical perceptions are subjectively indistinguishable, then the person must be aware of the same thing in both cases.
  - **C2** So, from C1, P2 and P3, what they are directly aware of during veridical perception must also be in the mind.
  - **C3** Hence we perceive the world indirectly and direct realism is false.

Response to this issue

- The fact that hallucinations can be subjectively indistinguishable from veridical perceptions (as in P3) doesn't show that they are the same phenomenon in reality.
- The direct realist may argue that hallucinations in fact have a very different causal history from veridical perceptions. Rather than being caused by a physical object impacting on the sense organs, hallucinations are produced by some sort of malfunction in the brain.
- Since hallucinations and veridical perceptions are not identical phenomena, even if they are indistinguishable to the person subject to them, it does not follow from the fact that hallucinations occur in the mind that veridical perceptions involve a purely mental element.

Issue: the time-lag argument

This argument is briefly outlined in Chapter 2 of Russell's *Problems of Philosophy*.

- It begins by pointing out that the light from the Sun takes a certain amount of time to travel to Earth – around eight minutes.
- So when you look up at the Sun, what you see is not the Sun as it is now but as it was some eight minutes ago. Indeed, Russell points out, if the Sun had ceased to exist within the last eight minutes, you wouldn't know about it yet.
- But if what you are seeing may no longer exist, then you cannot really be seeing it. That is, what you are seeing must be sense data caused in you by the Sun's light impacting on your visual system, and not the Sun itself.

- What is true of distant objects is no less true of objects close to, it's just that the time-lag is far shorter.
- So we can generalise and say that the immediate objects of perception are sense data, and our perception of all physical objects is indirect.
- Outline of the argument:

P1 The light from distant objects (such as the Sun) takes time to reach our eyes.

C1 So what we are seeing now may no longer exist.

C2 So what we are seeing and what is there are different.

P2 This is no less true for physical objects at any distance.

C3 And so, what we directly see are appearances not physical objects, and direct realism is false.

Response to this issue

The direct realist may argue that C1 doesn't imply C2. The time-lag means that what we are seeing is in the past and so it may have ceased to exist by the time we perceive it. But there is nothing in the direct realist view that commits it to the claim that the moment at which we perceive an object must be simultaneous with the object perceived. So the time-lag doesn't mean that we are seeing objects indirectly, it just means we are seeing them as they were. As Russell himself says 'when we see the Sun, we are seeing the Sun of eight minutes ago'.

- Part of the appeal of the time-lag argument may be the way it draws attention to the physical process that must occur in order for us to become aware of objects. It is undeniably true that light is mediating between us and the Sun.
- Moreover, there are physiological processes that must take place in our bodies and brains before we can become aware of objects around us, and all these processes take time.
- But such processes of mediation are not sense data and none of this implies that we are directly aware of sense data or that we must use sense data to infer the existence of objects.
- Instead we can say that once we become aware of an object we are aware of the object itself.

Indirect realism

Introduction

The four key arguments against direct realism outlined in the last section have led many philosophers to embrace **indirect realism**.

- Indirect realism remains a realist theory. So it retains the belief that material objects exist independently of the mind.
- However, it draws a distinction between the reality of these objects and the way they appear.
- So, there are three elements in perception. The perceiver, the real objects that they perceive, but also the appearance of these objects to the perceiver (see Figure 1.3).
- What we are directly aware of in this model are appearances, which Locke terms '**ideas**' and Russell 'sense data'. These are **representations** of reality.
- We must infer, on the basis of these sense data, the nature of that reality. Because perception involves this inference, it is indirect.

Exam tip

In five- and twelve-mark questions you may be asked to explain a philosophical argument such as those discussed above. To gain top marks you need to make clear how the different elements of the argument, the premises and the conclusions, fit together. In other words you need to be aware of the structure of the argument. Presenting the arguments in standard form is a clear and straightforward way of doing this. Having presented the argument in this manner, it is a good idea to explain the thinking to show full understanding, so that the examiner is clear that you have done more than simply memorise the steps.

Now test yourself

Set out all the arguments against direct realism in standard form.

TESTED ☐

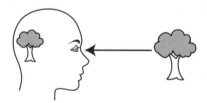

Figure 1.3 Indirect realism: we directly perceive sense data which are representations of reality.

Revision activity

Use an example of your own to explain the main tenets of direct realism.

Support for indirect realism

This revised picture of how perception works accounts for perceptual variations, illusions, hallucinations and the perceptual time-lag. For what we directly perceive need not always be an accurate representation of reality. Perceptual variations can occur while the real object remains unchanged; illusions occur when the appearance of an object doesn't match the reality; hallucinations when there is no real object corresponding to our sense data, and the time-lag can be explained because what I am immediately aware of is not the same as what is really there. So this looks like a clear strength of indirect over direct realism.

Locke's primary/secondary quality distinction

Locke's key definitions

Idea: 'Whatsoever the mind perceives in itself, or is the immediate object of perception, thought, or understanding, that I call idea.'

Qualities: 'the power to produce any idea in our mind I call a quality of the subject wherein that power is' (Essay, II, viii, 8).

According to Locke, there is another way in which reality does not precisely correspond with appearances. He argues that what he calls 'ideas' or sense data of certain properties of objects *resemble* their real properties. These are the **primary qualities**.

- So, when I look at a tree, for example, my sense data of its size, shape, position and motion correspond fairly accurately with its true size, shape, position and motion.
- But my sense data of its **secondary qualities**, such as its colour, taste and sound, do not.
- So whatever it is that causes me to see the leaves as green is not itself green.
- In other words, the property or quality of the leaves that causes a green sense datum in my mind does not resemble the sense datum.

Locke calls these secondary qualities 'powers' to produce an idea or sensation in us. These powers are a consequence of the movements and so on of the '**insensible** parts' of objects, that is of their microstructures, consisting of primary qualities, which we cannot directly observe.

Support for Locke's primary/secondary quality distinction

Primary qualities are essential

Locke argues that primary qualities are 'utterly inseparable' from an object, meaning that however the object is altered, such as when a grain of wheat is divided or an almond is pounded, its parts must retain some shape, size, position and so on, even if we can no longer see the parts. Without these qualities it wouldn't be material at all. Therefore, the primary qualities must be essential to material objects and are retained by the objects whether or not anyone perceives them.

This seems to be an *a priori* argument based on what we can conceive, summarised as follows:

P1 If you continually divide an object the parts must retain the primary qualities even when they are too small to be perceived.

C Therefore primary qualities must exist mind independently.

By contrast, secondary qualities do alter or vanish. Colours are only visible in the light and change depending on the light. A pounded almond changes its colour and taste. If we block our noses or ears, or don't place an object in our mouths, then it will not make a sound or have any odour or taste. So, Locke concludes, the secondary qualities both depend on the primary qualities and require a mind to appear and so are not in the objects themselves as we perceive them.

We can distinguish another argument in Locke as follows:

P1 When we pound an almond we merely change the shape of its parts.

P2 But the colour and taste of the almond also change.

C So, the change in colour and taste is caused by the change in the shape of the almond's parts.

Criticism

Locke's examples actually show that both the primary and the secondary qualities can change. When an almond is pounded, the shape of its parts changes, as does its taste, smell and colour. While the parts do retain some shape, the pounded almond also retains some taste, smell, and colour. So if change is supposed to show that a quality is secondary, by Locke's logic it seems we should regard the shape and size of the pieces of almond as mind-dependent. What is more, if we accept that the secondary qualities depend on the texture of the almond, this doesn't show that they are purely mind-dependent. Surely it is more reasonable to conclude that a certain taste, smell and colour are objective properties of pounded almond.

This argument also appears in Locke:

P1 Certain qualities disappear if we block our sense organs.

C So these qualities depend on our sense organs and do not exist as perceived in reality.

Criticism

This argument too appears to be unable to distinguish primary and secondary qualities. If we close our eyes, both the primary and the secondary qualities as perceived by us will disappear. While we can handle objects to feel their shapes, if we let go of them then those sense experiences cease (we stop feeling them). So it looks as though primary qualities behave the same as secondary in this regard.

Perceptual variation

Another argument Locke uses for the distinction involves an experiment of placing a warm and a cold hand into the same lukewarm water (see **page 16**). The water will feel hot and cold at the same time. But since the water itself cannot be hot and cold at the same time, the warmth must be a sensation produced in us by the movement of the minute particles of the water.

Outline of the argument:

P1 The same water can produce the idea (or sense datum) of cold to one hand and of warmth to the other.

P2 But the same thing cannot be both cold and warm at once.

C1 Therefore, the cold or warmth cannot belong to the material object (the water).

C2 So cold and warmth are purely sensations produced in the perceiver.

(Essay, Book II, ch.8 par. 21)

> **Exam tip**
>
> Berkeley offers his own arguments to undermine the Lockean distinction between primary and secondary qualities. Explore these when writing critically about the distinction in the exam (see **pages 24–25**).

Ideas or sense data	Matter and its qualities
What the perceiver is directly aware of in perception.	What the perceiver is indirectly aware of in perception.
They are mind-dependent.	Matter and its qualities are mind-independent.
Our ideas or sense data are caused by the qualities of matter.	The qualities of matter have the power to cause our ideas.
Ideas of primary qualities resemble the primary qualities of objects.	Primary qualities exist mind-independently.
Ideas of secondary qualities do not resemble the secondary qualities of objects.	Secondary qualities are powers to cause certain ideas as a result of the arrangement and movements of the insensible parts of matter. So secondary qualities are ultimately reducible to the primary. And secondary qualities are partly defined by their power to cause certain sensations in a perceiver.

> **Exam tip**
>
> It is common to confuse secondary qualities with sense data, as though we are immediately aware of secondary qualities and only indirectly aware of primary qualities. To avoid this sort of confusion, it may be helpful to remember that 'quality' is Locke's term for the properties of objects which cause ideas or sense data in us. So both sets of qualities exist in the material world. Our ideas/sense data include the perception of sounds, colours, tastes but also shapes, sizes, positions, and movements. In other words, our ideas/sense data are of both sets of qualities. The difference, therefore, is in the relationship between ideas and qualities.

Issues with indirect realism

Issue: scepticism about the existence of mind-independent objects

REVISED

The main difficulty for indirect realism is that it can lead to scepticism about the existence of the **external world**.

- According to indirect realism, we are directly aware only of sense data and must infer the existence of objects beyond the mind.
- However, our senses can deceive us.
- Worse, it is conceivable that our sense data do not correspond with any material reality, if, for example I am a brain in a vat or there is a powerful Cartesian demon bent on deceiving me.
- These possibilities show that the inference is not valid, and so not sufficient for knowledge.

Another way of making this point is to observe that we can only truly know what we are directly aware of. Since we cannot directly observe reality we cannot know that it exists. This is often called the 'veil of perception' problem for it is saying that our sense data constitute a veil between us and reality which we cannot penetrate to discover the material world.

Responses to this issue

The involuntary nature of our experience (Locke)

One response from Locke involves pointing out that we are not in control of our sense data. If I open my eyes I will receive certain sense data and this is not something I have any choice about. Because perception is not subject to my will, Locke argues, it cannot come from me. And therefore the source of sensation must be external.

The coherence of various kinds of experience (Locke, Cockburn)

A second Lockean argument appeals to the way our different senses cohere with each other.

- For example, Locke observes, we can both see a fire and feel its heat.
- Similarly it is possible to hear and to see a bus move.
- Catherine Trotter Cockburn also observes that we learn to associate the way objects feel to the touch and the way they appear to the eye. For example, if I recognise a dice by touch I can predict how it will look.
- I can also predict what I will perceive next. For example, if I close my eyes while writing, I can predict what words will appear when I open my eyes again, says Locke (IV, xi, 7).

In these ways the senses independently offer support for each other's testimony, suggesting that there is one external cause of both sets of perceptions.

Locke is aware that these are not deductively valid arguments.

- The fact that I cannot control my sense experiences and that they cohere with each other doesn't entail that they must be caused by material reality. This inference goes beyond the evidence.
- After all, when we dream, our sense experiences are often not subject to the will – I cannot always control my dreams. In a dream I may well appear to see, hear and feel the same objects. Despite this, dreams do not correspond with a material reality.
- However, here Locke hopes he has done enough to show that the inference to the existence of mind-independent objects is reasonable and as good as we, as creatures of limited faculties, can attain (Essay IV, xi, 7–8). The reality of matter is, he thinks, by far the best explanation of our experience than any alternative, such as that it is all a dream.

The external world is the 'best hypothesis' (Russell)

Russell also accepts that no deductive proof of the nature of a material reality is possible. But, like Locke, he still believes that scepticism can be resisted and also offers an argument to the best explanation or 'best hypothesis'. Russell's argument is that we have an instinctive belief in the existence of material reality which corresponds with our sense data and that we should only reject such instinctive beliefs if they are shown to be incoherent. So the onus is on the sceptic to show that belief in an external world is untenable. However, argues Russell, this belief is not at all contradictory and it actually makes very good sense of our experience. It explains why our sense data appear in regular and predictable ways, as Locke pointed out. Russell's discussion of his cat is used to illustrate the point.

Issue: ideas cannot be like material objects (Berkeley)

REVISED

However, Russell's argument only works if he is right that belief in the existence of material objects is not an incoherent one. But Berkeley argues that it is. After all, we only ever have direct awareness of our own sense data, and so, Berkeley urges, the very idea of a thing which we cannot be aware of is nonsensical. One of his arguments for this begins by observing that:

- All sense data, including those of so-called primary qualities, depend on the mind.

> **Revision activity**
>
> Read Locke's *Essay Concerning Human Understanding*, Book IV, Chapter xi (particularly sections 4–9). Outline each of the different arguments he uses to defend belief in the existence of the external world.

> **Revision activity**
>
> Read Russell's discussion of his cat in Chapter 2 of *The Problems of Philosophy* (Oxford: OUP, 1912, pages 10–11). Then explain his argument that the external world is the best hypothesis, using his cat example to illustrate.

Now test yourself answers at **www.hoddereducation.co.uk/myrevisionnotesdownloads**

- The qualities we perceive in objects, therefore, require a perceiving mind to exist.
- Since matter is said to be unperceiving, it cannot have such properties.

Another argument against indirect realism involves appeal to Berkeley's so-called 'likeness principle': the idea that ideas (or sense data) can only resemble other ideas and therefore we can make no sense of the claim that our ideas could be like or resemble the primary qualities of objects.

The argument can be set out as follows:

P1 My idea of, for example, a tree, has certain **sensible** qualities (for example, green, tree shaped, etc.).

P2 But these sensible qualities depend on the mind.

P3 To say that my idea of a tree resembles the real material tree is like saying something visible can resemble something invisible, or that a sound can resemble what is not a sound.

P4 Also ideas are fleeting and changing, whereas material objects are supposed to be permanent and unchanging.

C1 Thus anything outside of the mind (like matter) cannot have any such qualities.

C2 It follows that a supposed material object could not be *like* or *resemble* my idea of it.

Now test yourself

Recall the key arguments for and against indirect realism and present them in standard form.   TESTED

Berkeley's idealism

Introduction

The central claim of Berkeley's **idealism** can be easily summed up.

- All that exists are minds and their ideas.
- This means that what we call physical objects do not exist independently of being perceived. They are no more than collections of ideas or sense data appearing in minds.
- But Berkeley doesn't believe that objects exist only when perceived by finite human minds. Rather, he argues that the universe is sustained in existence through being perceived by the infinite mind of God.
- God directly causes our ideas or sense data.

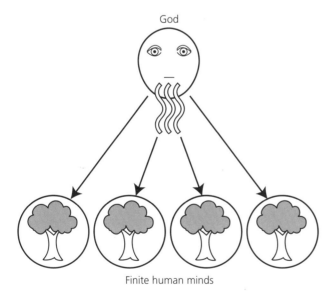

God

Finite human minds

Figure 1.4 Each finite mind is given perceptions directly by God. The perceptions in different minds are sufficiently similar and cohere with each other such that there is the appearance of us perceiving the same objects.

Revision activity

Use an example of your own to explain the main tenets of idealism.

Berkeley's attack on the primary/secondary distinction

Recall that, according to Locke, some of our ideas (sense data) resemble the objective properties of objects – their primary qualities – but our ideas of secondary qualities do not at all resemble what causes them. Berkeley tries to collapse this distinction in order to show that neither primary nor secondary qualities can be said to resemble anything beyond the mind.

Secondary qualities are not separable from primary qualities

Locke argued that no matter how often we divide a material object we cannot conceive of it without primary qualities (see **page 19**).
He concluded that these primary qualities are essential to an object. Berkeley responds that we are equally incapable of conceiving of an object without secondary qualities and therefore that these too must be essential to our idea of it.

- To show this, he asks us to try to imagine an object with only the primary qualities of size, shape and motion.
- But if we try to do this, he argues, we must imagine it with colour.
- He concludes that we cannot distinguish primary and secondary qualities in this way and that both are equally mind-dependent.
- This can be summarised as follows:

  P1 It is impossible to imagine an object with only the primary qualities of shape, size, movement, etc.

  C1 So our ideas of the so-called secondary qualities of an object cannot be separated from those of its primary qualities.

  C2 It follows that they must exist together.

  P2 Indirect realists accept that our ideas of secondary qualities are mind-dependent.

  C3 It follows that our ideas of primary qualities are also mind-dependent.

Support for indirect realism

- However, if we are careful to distinguish the ideas or sense data and the qualities of objects that cause them, then Berkeley's argument looks flawed.
- For Locke is *not* saying that secondary qualities themselves are mind-dependent. Rather, secondary qualities are the powers in objects to cause sensations in us and they are mind-independent.
- So the fact that both the primary and secondary qualities as perceived by me seem inseparable doesn't mean that both sets of qualities themselves must exist in the mind.
- Rather, the sense data of primary and of secondary qualities exist in the mind, but the qualities themselves exist mind-independently.

Perceptual variation

Locke used the perceptual variation argument to show that certain perceived qualities cannot exist in material objects as we perceive them (see **page 20**). Berkeley tries to run a parallel argument for the primary qualities arguing that size, shape, and movement are also subject to perceptual relativity and so cannot be considered as real properties of external objects.

Now test yourself answers at **www.hoddereducation.co.uk/myrevisionnotesdownloads**

Here are outlines of these arguments from *Dialogue 1*.

P1 What looks small to us will look big to a mite.

P2 A material object cannot be small and big at the same time.

C Therefore size cannot be a property of material objects.

P1 The perceived shape of an object changes depending on the angle of observation.

P2 But an object cannot have different shapes at the same time.

C Therefore shape cannot be a property of material objects

P1 The speed of an object may appear fast or slow to different minds (perhaps because you are bored and I am not, or to a bird as compared to a human).

P2 But the motion of an external object cannot be both fast and slow at the same time.

C So the motion is not a property of external objects.

Berkeley's conclusion is that the primary qualities are mind-dependent, just like the secondary qualities.

Criticism

- The indirect realist can resist Berkeley's use of perceptual variation to try to show that there are no mind-independent qualities of objects.
- The first two premises of these arguments can be accepted for it is true that the way we perceive both primary and secondary qualities can vary depending on the position and so forth of the perceiver.
- But it doesn't follow that the qualities themselves which indirect realists claim cause our ideas cannot be mind-independent.
- If we distinguish the apparent size, shape and speed from the real size, shape or speed, we can draw a different conclusion.
- So indirect realists will insist that this is the legitimate inference to draw:
  P1 The apparent size, shape or motion of an object varies.
  P2 A material object's objective properties cannot vary.
  C Therefore the *apparent* size, shape and motion cannot be objective properties of material objects. But a material object can still have some specific size, shape and motion independent of the mind.

Berkeley's 'master' argument

REVISED

Berkeley's 'master' argument tries to show that the very idea of a mind-independent material object is contradictory and so impossible:

P1 Try to conceive of a tree which exists independent of any mind.

P2 In doing so, the tree is being conceived by you.

C Therefore the tree is in your mind and not independent of any mind after all.

Criticism

A standard objection to this argument can be found in one of the anthology texts, Russell's *Problems of Philosophy* Chapter 4. Russell argues that Berkeley's error is to confuse the mental act of conceiving a thing with the thing being conceived. So it is true that my idea of a tree must be in my mind, but it doesn't follow that what my idea is about, namely the tree itself, must be in my mind.

Another objection is that Berkeley's argument, if valid, would prove too much. It would show that I could not make sense of the idea of anything existing outside of my mind. In this case, it would mean that only my mind could exist and so would lead directly to **solipsism** (see page 27). Berkeley's appeal to God as the eternal perceiver would thus be undermined and so his whole system defeated.

Criticism of Berkeley's likeness principle

- Berkeley doesn't explain precisely why he thinks an idea can only be like another idea. But certainly part of his thought is that without being able to compare our ideas with reality we have no way of establishing any such resemblance.
- However, defenders of indirect realism might appeal to the arguments for the existence of an external world that we have already examined, such as that it is the best explanation of our experience. If we accept that a material world is the cause of our ideas, then it seems reasonable to suppose that there will be a systematic correlation between reality and our perception of it.

Now test yourself

See if you can outline Berkeley's argument against indirect realism which appeals to his 'likeness principle'. Explain how this argument supports idealism.

TESTED

Issues with Berkeley's idealism

Issue: arguments from illusions and hallucinations

REVISED

- Idealism says that all physical things depend on the mind to exist. Common sense says that imagined things depend on the mind, but real things are importantly different. Normally this difference is understood as being to do with their mind-independent existence. So how does the idealist distinguish imagined from real objects?
- Berkeley's response is that we can distinguish objects of the imagination because firstly they are subject to the will: I am in control of conjuring them into existence. Moreover, when I imagine a tree it is far less vivid and clear than when I actually perceive one.
- However, this still leaves a similar worry about how to characterise illusions and hallucinations. For realists, this distinction is relatively straightforward: illusions occur when our mind-dependent sense data mislead us about mind-independent reality. Hallucinations occur when there is nothing in reality corresponding with the sense data.
- But if there is no mind-independent reality, then illusions and hallucinations would appear to be no different from veridical perceptions and this certainly doesn't fit well with our common sense.
- Berkeley's response is to argue that, when subject to an illusion, I am not mistaken about the actual sense data or ideas. An illusion and a hallucination are subjectively indistinguishable from other sense experiences and it would be nonsense to say we can be wrong about these. However, the reason we regard them as illusory is because they incline us to make false inferences about what we may perceive next.
- So, if I judge on the basis of seeing an oar appear half bent in water that it will also feel bent to the touch, then I will be making an error. Similarly, if I try to grab a dagger which I see before me but clutch only thin air, then I have been fooled by a hallucination. The error in both cases lies in the inference made about further sense data because I judged I would have certain tactile sensations which were not forthcoming.

Now test yourself answers at **www.hoddereducation.co.uk/myrevisionnotesdownloads**

Issue: idealism leads to solipsism

- If ideas of sensible qualities of objects must exist in the mind, then it seems I cannot know of the existence of any reality beyond it. The 'master argument' goes further. It concludes that the very idea of a mind-independent object is self-contradictory and so impossible. But if Berkeley's reasoning is correct it seems to imply that the world first appeared only when I was born, will disappear when I die, and comes in and out of existence every time I blink my eyes.
- However, this objection ignores the role of God in Berkeley's complete theory. Berkeley doesn't claim that things can only exist in *my* mind, but that they must exist in *some* mind. And he claims that God is a permanent perceiver of the universe when no finite human or animal mind is perceiving it. In this way, objects retain the kind of permanence that common sense would demand.
- However, the worry may be pressed further to question whether we can make sense of the idea of God for, Berkeley argues, minds can only be aware of their ideas. Since a mind is the possessor of ideas, it is not itself an idea and so, strictly speaking, we cannot have an idea of a mind. But in this case we cannot have the idea of God's mind, or indeed of any other minds, so we are plunged back into solipsism.

Berkeley's response

- Berkeley's response is to admit that I cannot have an idea of God's mind. God's mind is not the sort of thing which has sensible qualities and so is not something I can frame in my mind.
- However, he says, I can form a 'notion' of it by 'intuition' or 'reflection' on myself. As Descartes argued in the *Meditations*, Berkeley claims I am aware that there is a **self** which possesses my ideas. This self is something unextended and indivisible.
- Berkeley thinks he has satisfactorily proved that God must exist as the cause of my ideas and as what sustains the universe in existence. And so I can extend this 'notion' of myself by enlarging my own powers and subtracting my imperfections to produce a notion of the mind of God.

Issue: problems with the role played by God in Berkeley's idealism

It is common for students to complain that Berkeley uses God to overcome the problems with his view that matter doesn't exist, and that since there is no proof that God exists we can reject his appeal to divine intervention and the theory of idealism with it. As it stands this objection betrays a misunderstanding of Berkeley's reasoning and so care needs to be taken in how to make the point.

To see this it's important to recall that Berkeley believes he has demonstrated that the philosophical idea of matter is incoherent. He also thinks that the only source of our sense data must be something that can itself possess sense data and which has the active power to cause them in us. Matter can do neither because it is not sentient or active. But he also agrees with Locke and Russell that the regularity and predictability of our sense data, the fact that they are not subject to my will and that the different senses cohere with each other, all show that the source of them is external to me. His conclusion is, therefore, that the source of sense data must be a mind, and a very powerful mind. So he doesn't consider himself to have brought in God to save his theory. Rather his arguments have inexorably led to the existence of God as the only possible explanation of our experience (*Third Dialogue*).

So, be sure to show you are aware of Berkeley's strategy when objecting to his use of God. The objection can then be made that Berkeley's appeal to God is not, as he insists, a better explanation of our experience than matter. Matter may be defended as the better explanation because it gives a better account of illusions and hallucinations and of the underlying processes which bring about our sense experiences.

Can God have sensations?

Another objection to Berkeley's use of God explored in the *Third Dialogue* is that to say that God perceives all and is the source of our sense experience implies that he is subject to sensations, including pain, and he cannot, therefore, be perfect.

The argument may be outlined as follows:
P1 Berkeley claims that what we perceive is in the mind of God.
C1 It follows that the idea of pain is in the mind of God; in other words God suffers pain.
P2 But if God suffers pain, then he is imperfect.
P3 God is defined as a perfect being.
C2 Therefore Berkeley's views lead to a contradiction.

Berkeley's own response is that while God knows what it is for us to suffer pain, he doesn't suffer it himself. Philonous says, 'God knows or has ideas; but his ideas aren't conveyed to him by sense as ours are' (*Third Dialogue*). In other words, in the case of humans we suffer because pains are caused in us in accordance with the laws of nature and we have no control over them. But God doesn't have a body and so God does not suffer from pain or other sensations against his will. Because he is a pure spirit and actively determines his ideas he cannot be said to passively 'suffer' from pain or any other sensation.

However, arguably there remains a problem for Berkeley. For sensations are fleeting and changing. The world perceived by God is also one of change. If God has sensations, then he must change. And if he changes then he cannot be perfect and immutable.

> **Exam tip**
>
> Five- or twelve-mark questions may ask you to identify or explain the key differences between two of these theories of perception. A good way to revise the details of the theories and to prepare for such questions is to pair up two theories and draw up a list of similarities and/or differences.

Differences between idealism and indirect realism	
Idealism	**Indirect realism**
Idealism is an **anti-realist** theory and indirect realism is a form of **realism**. That is, the former claims that objects are mind-dependent and denies the existence of mind-independent material objects.	Indirect realism claims that material objects exist beyond perception.
Berkeley's idealism is a direct theory of perception. Physical objects are clusters of sensible qualities directly perceived by the mind.	Indirect realists argue that we perceive the qualities of matter but that these qualities inhere in a material substratum which is not directly perceived. Thus the existence and nature of material objects must be inferred from their representations in the mind.
Berkeley explains the regularity and predictability of our sense experience and the persistence of objects unperceived by finite minds by appeal to the mind of God as a permanent perceiver and the source of our perceptions.	Indirect realists argue that matter is the best explanation of experience.
For idealism ideas cannot be like anything but other ideas.	For indirect realists our sense data/ideas are representations of material reality.
Berkeley tries to collapse the distinction between primary and secondary qualities.	Traditionally, indirect realism distinguishes primary from secondary qualities

Exam checklist

You should be able to:	✓
Explain the main tenets of direct realism and its advantages	
Outline the four key arguments against direct realism and assess how effective they are:	
● the argument from illusion	
● the argument from perceptual variation	
● the argument from hallucination	
● the time-lag argument	
Explain the main tenets of indirect realism and its advantages	
Explain Locke's primary/secondary quality distinction and his arguments for it. Assess how effective they are	
Explain the difficulties for indirect realism:	
● that it leads to scepticism about the external world	
● how Berkeley's likeness principle undermines indirect realism.	
Explain defences against this scepticism:	
● the involuntary nature of our experience (Locke)	
● the coherence of the senses (Locke, Cockburn)	
● the best hypothesis (Russell)	
Explain the main tenets of Berkeley's idealism and its advantages	
Explain the arguments for idealism and assess how effective they are:	
● the attack on the primary/secondary quality distinction	
● the master argument	
Explain the problems for Berkeley's idealism:	
● how to explain illusions and hallucination	
● his use of God to explain regularity and predictability	
● the difficulty that God cannot experience sensations	

Reason as a source of knowledge

Introduction

What are the ultimate sources of our knowledge? God, experience, reason?

Empiricism

Empiricist philosophers claim that experience and evidence from the senses provide us with most, if not all, of our knowledge.

Rationalism

Rationalists claim that reason, by itself, can be a source of knowledge. The suggestion is that alone in a room, cut off from the world, in theory it should be possible to work out substantial truths about the world using reason alone.

The distinction between knowing something through experience or independently of experience (usually through reason) is captured by the Latin terms, *a posteriori* and *a priori*. Recall the JTB definition of knowledge – these two terms relate to the J element. If the *justification* for a truth or belief is dependent on experience then the knowledge is *a posteriori*. If it can be justified independently of experience then it is *a priori*.

A priori knowledge	*A posteriori* knowledge
Justification is independent of experience	Justification is based on experience
Known with certainty in advance of experience	Cannot be known with certainty in advance of experience
For example: 2 + 3 = 5	For example: France won the World Cup in 2018

Innatism

Innatism is the claim that we are born with knowledge. Innatists usually believe this knowledge can be revealed through reason.

Plato was puzzled by the relationship between concepts and individual instances. For example, we seem to have a concept of beauty, but never witness beauty in its pure form, only imperfectly in different people and objects. So, what is beauty itself?

Plato claimed that in a prior existence, we apprehended these perfect concepts or '**forms**' in their pure state. We have forgotten most of these forms, but they are in us innately. Plato believed that through reasoning we can achieve a perfect understanding/apprehension once again.

Plato's account contains some classic features of innatism:

A **Innate ideas** are 'in' us, although we might not be aware of them (like a forgotten memory is 'in' us).

B We can realise these innate ideas through reason.

C Innate ideas provide timeless truths.

> **Exam tip**
>
> Three-mark questions often ask you explain what a term or idea means. Clearly (and succinctly) answer these questions: What is innatism? What is *a priori* knowledge? What is *a posteriori* knowledge?

Now test yourself answers at **www.hoddereducation.co.uk/myrevisionnotesdownloads**

Plato's argument from the 'slave boy'

In the *Meno*, Plato shows how a slave boy can access his innate ideas.

Plato's argument might be summarised as follows:
P1 The slave boy has no prior knowledge of geometry/squares.
P2 Socrates only asks questions; he does not teach the boy about squares.
P3 After the questioning, the slave boy can grasp an eternal truth about geometry/squares.
P4 This eternal truth was not derived from the boy's prior experience, nor from Socrates.
C This eternal truth must have existed innately in the boy to begin with.

Criticism: memory or the faculty of reason?

Perhaps the slave is simply using reason to work out what must be the case given certain features of lines and shapes. It is not necessary to posit innate knowledge to explain how the boy can reason his way to the discovery of a geometric truth.

Innate ideas: Leibniz

Leibniz believed that the human mind could gain knowledge of the world through reason alone (though prompted by the senses). His belief also rests on the claim that we have innate ideas – which he called 'principles' – which are revealed by reason.

Argument from the necessity of truth

Leibniz argued that there are different kinds of truths, some of which he termed necessary. We see the Sun rise every day (an instance), from this we make a general truth (via induction) that *the Sun rises every day.* This is revealed by the senses, but it is not a necessary truth. One day the Sun may cease to exist.

Contrast this with mathematical truths such as $2 + 3 = 5$. Our mind sees that this will always be the case. It is a necessary truth. The 'necessity' of a truth cannot be revealed by the senses, but only reason – which is the application of principles that are innately inside us.

Formally, the argument might be summarised as follows:
P1 The senses only reveal instances of general truths.
P2 The senses cannot reveal the necessity of a general truth.
P3 Our minds can see the necessity of some general truths.
C Our ability to see the necessity of general truth is not derived from the senses, but is based on innate principles.

For Leibniz innate ideas/principles include: truths of mathematics; logical principles such as the law of non-contradiction (for example, an object cannot be blue and not blue at the same time); the concept of identity.

Leibniz did **not** claim that innate principles exist within us fully formed from birth. Our mind is like a block of marble which has 'veins' running through it in such a way that it will readily take a specific shape. The marble does not contain the fully formed statue but has the 'inclination' or 'tendency' to take the shape when struck. Likewise, we are not born with innate ideas fully formed – our minds are structured such that certain ideas and principles will appear once prompted by the senses (though not derived from the senses).

Empiricist responses

Locke's arguments against innate ideas

John Locke was an empiricist. At the time of his writing, innatism was a commonly held belief and he provided several arguments against this.

1. No universal assent

People claimed that because some ideas are held by everyone, they must be innate. Locke attacked this idea, by claiming that children (and idiots) do not possess some allegedly innate principles such as 'whatever is, is' (the law of identity) and 'it is impossible for the same thing to be and not to be' (the law of non-contradiction).

Formally, his argument might be summarised as follows:
P1   Any innate idea, x, if it exists, would be universally held.
P2   Children and idiots do not have the idea of x.
P3   If an idea is held in the mind then you must be aware of it. (This is the *transparency argument* – see below.)
C1   So x is not universally held.
C2   Therefore x is not innate.

Criticism (issue with this response)

Leibniz claims (against P2) that 'children and idiots' *do* actually employ innate principles in their everyday actions, even if they can't articulate the ideas in words. For example, a child knows her teddy cannot be in her hand and in the loft at the same time.

2. Transparency of ideas

Another argument against P2 is that 'children and idiots' might possess innate ideas but are not yet aware of them. To counter this Locke argues that if we did have innate ideas – such as the idea of God – then they must be present in our minds (P3) – not constantly, but we must have been conscious of them at some point. He claims our minds are transparent and we can perceive all the ideas they contain. After all, if you've never had an idea/thought, then in what sense can it be 'in' your mind?

Criticism (issue with this response)

Perhaps there *are* ideas/memories 'in' your mind that you have never been conscious of.
● Maybe you 'absorbed' a song on the radio, without being consciously aware of it. That song is not 'transparent' in your mind, but it may be recognisable if you heard it again. So, it must be 'in' you somewhere.
● Likewise, an innate idea could be 'in' your mind, without you being aware of it yet. Leibniz puts forward this idea in his *New Essays*.

3. How can we distinguish innate ideas from other ideas?

Locke argues that if some of our ideas are innate and some gained from experience, how can we tell them apart? Why not say the idea of blue was in you from birth, but only when you saw the colour blue does the idea/capacity become active? Likewise, with the idea of a cat or geometry etc.

Criticism (issue with this response)

Leibniz suggests that we *can* distinguish innate ideas from non–innate ones because they are true in a different way – they are *necessarily* true. Although young children may not know many of the truths of mathematics, once they do understand a truth, the mind immediately recognises that it has an eternal application and that such truths are different from truths of fact.

The mind as *tabula rasa*

REVISED

Locke's main argument against innatism is his claim that the mind is born 'empty' like a *tabula rasa* (meaning blank slate) and he can show how all our ideas/concepts are derived from the senses/experience. So, the theory of innate ideas is unnecessary. This argument relies on Ockham's razor (if competing explanations explain some phenomenon equally well, go for the simpler one).

Sense impressions and concepts

Locke (and Hume) argue that our minds receive impressions from the senses and that these are then copied into ideas or concepts. These ideas allow us to think about things that are not present to our senses. For example, I can think about cheese even though I am not currently in the presence of any cheese.

We can also combine simple ideas in our minds to create complex ideas which may have no corresponding impression (for example, a unicorn), but the elements (white, horse, horn) all must derive from actual impressions.

Input from the senses	Causes	Our minds
Simple impressions, e.g. smell	→	Simple idea/concept e.g. idea of red
		Can create ↑ ↓ Can break down to
Complex impressions, e.g. a painting	→	Complex ideas, e.g. a unicorn

Revision activity

Summarise Locke's arguments against innatism. What counter-arguments does Leibniz provide against Locke's arguments?

This theory can be used to attack innatism. The argument may be presented as follows:
P1 The theory of innate ideas claims we are born with innate ideas.
P2 All of our ideas can be shown to be derived from experience (*tabula rasa*).
C The theory of innate ideas is redundant.

Support for the *tabula rasa* theory

- People born lacking a sense (for example, lacking impressions of, say, red) also lack the corresponding ideas (red).
- Can you imagine a new idea (for example, a gold mountain) that is not ultimately derived from impressions you have experienced (gold + mountain)?

Criticism (issues with the *tabula rasa* response)

Do all ideas come from impressions?

Maybe I can create a new shade of blue in my mind by merging ones I already have. This new simple idea/shade has not come from a simple impression. Also, I can have the concept of ultraviolet light without having experienced it.

Relational concepts

What about concepts such as sameness? 'Sameness' does not have a particular colour or taste. 'Sameness' cannot be related to any *specific* impressions. Do we derive the concept of 'sameness' from our impressions? Or do we have it innately, prior to experience?

Concepts needed for experience

Kant argues that we experience the world as a series of *objects* in *space* and *time* interacting in *causal* ways because your experience has the concepts such as *unity*, *space*, *time* and *causation* already applied to it (by you). **Sense impressions** (which he terms intuitions) prior to any form of conceptual ordering cannot yet form any part of any experience. We have existing (innate) concepts that enable experience to happen.

Chomsky (1928–) has argued that our minds must have innate structures in place to learn language so efficiently as children.

Hume's fork

If the *tabula rasa* theory is correct, then we are not born with innate ideas. If so, then all our ideas and most/if not all our knowledge must come from experience.

In *An Enquiry Concerning Human Understanding*, Hume gives an account of knowledge in relation to reason and experience. He divides the areas of human understanding into two distinct camps: relations of ideas and matters of fact.

Relations of ideas

- Revealed by reason, these concern logic, mathematics and the relations between concepts (though sense experience is needed to form concepts).
- The opposite of a true relation of ideas is not just false but is a contradiction (this enables them to be 'proven' by deduction).
- They do not depend on how the world actually is. Two and three will always make five – no need to check this by observing facts (it would still be true even if there were no objects).
- Because these truths are not derived from observing the world, Hume claims they do not tell us anything new about the world.

Matters of fact

- 'Matters of fact' can only be derived from experiencing how the world is.
- It may seem obvious that (most) objects fall downwards or that fire burns, but this is only known through experience.
- Hume claims that our knowledge in this area consists of a) observing how the world is, and b) generalising from experience (induction).
- Matters of fact can never be certain; we can only achieve degrees of probability. We may feel absolutely certain that the Sun will rise tomorrow – but maybe it will not.

	Relations of ideas (prong one of fork)	Matters of fact (prong two of fork)
Covers	Mathematics, geometry, logic	Facts and generalisations about the world
Examples	2 + 4 = 6	Donald Trump was a US president
Certainty level	Absolute	Not 100 per cent certain. Level of probability
How we know	By thinking about the concepts alone (a priori)	By experience (a posteriori)
Reliance on how the world is	None: truth does not rely on how the world is	Complete reliance on how the world is
Is the opposite conceivable?	No – it is true by definition	Yes – the opposite is conceivable. Not true by definition
Type of truth	Analytic (a term coined later by Kant). Truth can be determined by thinking about the concepts alone	Synthetic truth. Truth cannot be determined by concepts alone. Evidence is needed

Hume realised that his 'fork' had powerful consequences for the writings of rationalist philosophers including Descartes. It suggests that substantial knowledge (i.e. not true by definition) cannot be generated by reason alone. In fancy terms, synthetic a priori knowledge is not possible. Rationalists, including Descartes, had tried to use reason alone to show how the world must be. According to Hume, these rationalists were wasting their time.

- Reason can only tell us things that are true by definition. All other 'substantial' knowledge has to be gained by experiencing the world.
- Once we have observed the world, reason may be able to help us deduce some further elements and truths, but by itself reason cannot tell us about the world.

Now test yourself

TESTED

Describe the two prongs of Hume's fork and say what implications it might have for rationalism.

The intuition and deduction thesis

Introduction

Prior to Hume and his fork, many rationalists argued that knowledge of the world could be based on reason alone. You start by establishing undeniable truths by reason and then use deduction to produce further truths.

Intuition, deduction and 'clear and distinct ideas' (Descartes)

REVISED

Inspired by the geometrical proofs of Euclid, Descartes devised four rules for gaining knowledge:

1 Accept only beliefs that can be recognised *clearly and distinctly* to be true.
2 Break problems down into the smallest parts.
3 Build up the arguments systematically in the right order (deduction).
4 Carefully check to ensure no steps are left out.

The big idea is that we can arrive at **clear and distinct ideas**, which the mind intuits are true. Then by using deduction the mind can arrive at further truths.

For Descartes, an idea is *clear* if is very bright and present to the mind. An idea is *distinct* if it is sharply separated from other ideas.

● He gives the example of a leg pain, which might be very *clear* to one afflicted, but is not *distinct*, as it may be hard to distinguish the pain from the true cause. The sufferer may be wrong about what is causing it.
● Examples of ideas that are both clear and distinct are *I am thinking* and *two and three make five*.

The Latin term *intueri* means to 'look upon'. So, by *intuition*, Descartes means an act of the intellect whereby it inwardly 'looks upon' an intellectual object, such as a straight line or a triangle, and instantly sees its true features.

You may find it useful to think of an *intuition* as one of the key operations of the mind, and a *clear and distinct idea* as the object 'perceived' by the intuition. So, for example, '*two and three make five*' would be the clear and distinct idea which the mind intuits is true.

Criticism: terms are not clear and distinct enough

Leibniz criticised Descartes, suggesting that a more detailed account of 'clear and distinct' is needed if these terms are to be used as criteria of truth. Relying on a feeling is not enough. Descartes does not give a sufficiently clear and distinct account of what is clear and distinct!

Criticism: quick generalisation

Descartes puts the success of the **cogito** down to the fact that its truth can be grasped clearly and distinctly. He then generalises this principle and claims that any belief he can conceive clearly and distinctly must also be true. But is this a valid generalisation to make?

Criticism: only internal criteria for truth

The correspondence theory of truth suggests a belief (internal to you) is true when it corresponds to a fact (external to you). However, Descartes claims we can tell if a belief is true using internal means alone (how clear and distinct it is). Ryle suggests this approach is mistaken – a bit like working out if you have scored a goal just by checking how well you kicked the ball (not by seeing whether it goes in).

> **Exam tip**
>
> For a five-mark question you may be asked to explain what Descartes meant by a clear and distinct idea. This is not easy to do unless you have practised it.

Now test yourself answers at **www.hoddereducation.co.uk/myrevisionnotesdownloads**

The *cogito* (*a priori* intuition)

In the *Meditations*, Descartes doubts his beliefs until he finally reaches a point of certainty. He concludes that he cannot be deceived about his existence. This seems to be a clear example of knowledge that is produced by reason alone.

> So after thoroughly thinking the matter through I conclude that this proposition, I am, I exist, must be true whenever I assert it or think it.
>
> Descartes, *Meditations*, Meditation 2, p.4.

To many it seems undeniably true that they must exist whenever they think about it, but how exactly does the *cogito* work?

A deduction?

The *cogito* could be presented as a **deductive argument** – something like this:

P1 I am thinking.
P2 (hidden premise) All thinking things exist.
C Therefore I exist.

Descartes explicitly denies the *cogito* is a deduction, but rather 'a simple intuition of his mind shows it to him as self-evident'. In the *Meditations*, Descartes needs the *cogito* to work as a simple intuition (rather than a longer argument) as he is still working under the assumption that a demon may be deceiving him, and this could affect the validity of his memory (which is required in a longer argument).

A transcendental argument?

Transcendental arguments attempt to 'transcend' doubt. They work by arguing that a certain feature (in this case existence) is a pre-condition for doubt to exist. If so, you cannot doubt you exist, as you need to exist in order to doubt. This seems a plausible approach, but again might be too complex to count as a single intuition, which Descartes may need to overcome the demon challenge.

A self-verifying thought?

Descartes often emphasises the temporary, fleeting nature of the *cogito*: 'I am, I exist, must be true whenever I assert it or think it.' This suggests that the truth of the *cogito* is revealed in the very act of performing it. The thought that 'I do **not** exist' is self-defeating in its performance – it is an assertoric inconsistency. In this way the thought 'I am, I exist' may be self-verifying because asserting the opposite is self-defeating.

Does the *cogito* produce knowledge?

What is the 'I' that is thinking?

If Descartes can only be sure he exists when he is actually thinking about it, is it possible that he may cease to exist when he is not thinking about it? Maybe every time the 'I am, I exist' is thought, it is a different person thinking it – perhaps created anew that second and given the memories of Descartes. Perhaps there is no self – no 'I' at all – just floating thoughts. It is not clear that the *cogito* has produced any knowledge in regard of the nature or even existence of the 'I' that is thinking.

Is the *cogito a priori* knowledge produced via intuition?

The *cogito* seems to be an example of substantial knowledge that is produced via reason alone, although Descartes, in the second set of objections and replies to the *Meditations*, presents it as some kind of induction 'what actually happens is that he learns it [the *cogito*] by experiencing in his own case that it isn't possible to think without existing'. However, if you take the idea that the *cogito* is a self-justifying thought, then it can be known independently of experience, so is *a priori*.

Revision activity

In different books Descartes expresses the *cogito* in different ways. Read the relevant section of the *Meditations*. Can you outline how Descartes expresses the *cogito* in the book? How does he argues for it?

Arguments for the existence of God (*a priori* deductions)

REVISED

Partly to escape his doubts, Descartes produced several arguments for the existence of a God (a good God who would not make a human such that her clearest and most distinct thoughts were false ones).

Trademark argument

Descartes' first argument is a good example of his intuition and deduction thesis in action.

From his initial clear and distinct idea of God and himself (intuitions), Descartes attempts to deduce God's existence. Descartes argues that his idea of God can only have appeared in his mind if there really is a God.

Formally his argument might be summarised as follows:

P1 The cause of anything must be at least as perfect as its effect.
P2 My ideas must be caused by something.
P3 I am an imperfect being.
P4 I have the idea of God, which is that of a perfect being.
IC1 (intermediate conclusion) I cannot be the cause of my idea of God (from P1, P2, P3 and P4).
IC2 Only a perfect being (that is, God) can be the cause of my idea of God (from P1 and P4).
C God must exist (from P4 and IC2).

Empiricist responses

Criticism: causal principle

Descartes believed it self-evidently true that the '*total cause of something must contain at least as much reality as does the effect*'. This causal principle may be true with regards to the physical world (it is similar to the first law of thermodynamics) but it is not clear how it would apply to the world of ideas. Our minds can easily create better versions of real objects. Indeed, Hume argued that our idea of God is derived from considering virtues in other people and augmenting them without limit.

Criticism: not *a priori*

Hume argued that we can never deduce the effect from examining the cause, or the cause from examining the effect. We need experience of causes and effects conjoined before we can learn of their connection. So, from knowing the effect, the idea of God, we cannot deduce what may have caused it. Broader causal theories – such as the 'causal principle' – also, can only be known through experience.

Criticism: idea of perfection

Some would argue that we do not have a clear idea of a perfect God or of infinity. If these concepts are not present in our minds, then Descartes' argument is undermined.

Contingency argument

Here Descartes argues that his own existence is enough to prove there is a God.

Formally, his argument might be summarised as follows:

P1 The cause of my existence as a thinking thing must be a) myself, b) I have always existed, c) my parents, or d) God.

P2 I cannot have caused myself to exist for then I would have created myself perfect.

P3 Neither have I always existed, for then I would be aware of this.

P4 My parents may be the cause of my physical existence, but not of me as a thinking mind.

C (by elimination) Therefore, only God could have created me.

Criticism

Could we have been created by a less than perfect being? Could we not have been created by another conscious being less great than God – perhaps an evil scientist, an angel or even a process of **evolution**? Why must our author be either ourselves, our parents or a perfect being (God)? After all, these options are not exhaustive (not the only ones).

Empiricist response

Criticism: Not *a priori*

- Both the trademark and the contingency arguments start from a state of affairs in the world and attempt to deduce the cause. In this way they both resemble abductive arguments, but by (allegedly) eliminating all other possibilities – they attempt to 'deduce' the only possible cause. Because they start from observations about how the world is (e.g. having an idea of God), they should be classed as *a posteriori* deductions.
- Again, Hume would argue that the reliance on the causal principle would undermine their status as deductions, as cause and effects are inductive generalisations.

Ontological argument

Later in the *Meditations*, Descartes argues that his mind can take any intelligible object and work out which features are essential to it. He attempts this with his idea of God, which is the idea of a supremely perfect being. To be perfect God must have all perfections, and this includes the property of existence. Therefore, God must exist.

Formally, his argument might be summarised as follows:

P1 I have an idea of God, as a perfect being.

P2 A perfect being must have all perfections.

P3 Existence is a perfection.

C God exists.

Criticism: 'the perfect island'

Gaunilo questioned an earlier version of the ontological argument, suggesting that, by the same logic, the perfect island must also exist (as existence is a perfection). This seems ridiculous. Descartes might argue back that the idea of an island is not like that of God. An island is not an intelligible object in the same way a triangle is, so we cannot discover its features just by thinking. Also, the idea of a perfect island will differ between minds. However, it can be argued back again that the concept of God is also not like a triangle. It is vague, not intelligible and also differs between minds.

Criticism: existence is not a predicate

A criticism put forward by many including Kant, Russell and Gassendi is that existence is not a quality of an object — it is not a **predicate**. Gassendi argues, 'What doesn't exist has no perfections or imperfections; what does exist may have various perfections, but existence won't be one of them.' If existence is not a predicate this undermines Descartes' argument which is based on existence being a quality of God, in the same way that omnipotence may be.

Empiricist response

Criticism: Hume's fork

Hume argued that claims about the existence of any object will always be *matters of fact*. As such, any claim will need investigation to discover its truth, not just reason as Descartes is attempting.

> Nothing is demonstrable unless its contrary implies a contradiction. Nothing that is distinctly conceivable implies a contradiction. Whatever we conceive as existent, we can also conceive as nonexistent. So there is no being whose non-existence implies a contradiction. So there is no being whose existence is demonstrable.
> Hume, *Dialogue*, part 9

According to Hume's fork, the most that Descartes' ontological argument could show is that the idea of God contains the idea of existence. However, this does not actually tell us if God exists.

Is this *a priori* knowledge?

Unlike the trademark and contingency arguments, the ontological argument seems to be based purely on the idea of God and is not based on any observation of the world. As such, if it works, then the existence of God can be said to be known *a priori*. However, there are problems with the argument.

> **Exam tip**
>
> You may have studied the ontological argument in Unit 3 of the A-level. If a question on Descartes' ontological argument occurs in the Unit 1 paper, make sure you articulate **Descartes'** version of the argument. You may need to memorise this.

Proof of the external world (*a priori* deduction)

REVISED

Proving the existence of the external world is not easy. Some, including Berkeley, claim that the belief in the existence of an external, material world is simply not justified.

Descartes' proof attempts to show that his sensations of objects cannot come from inside him and must be caused by the external world. His argument is in two steps:

Step 1a, b: *Sensations come from outside him* (Descartes produces two arguments for this).

1a:

P1 The will is a part of my essence.

P2 Sensation is not subject to my will.

C Sensations come from outside of me.

1b:

P1 My nature or essence is unextended.

P2 Sensations are ideas of extended things.

C Sensations come from outside of me.

Step 2: *Sensations originate from matter.*

P1 There are two possible sources for the origin of sensation: God or matter.

P2 I have a strong natural inclination to believe they come from matter, and I have no faculty by which to correct this belief.

IC So if their origin were in God, God would be a deceiver.

P3 God is not a deceiver.

C Sensation originates in matter.

Empiricist responses

Criticism of step 1a

Perhaps sensations come from a part of me of which I am not conscious. After all, dreams are not subject to our will any more than our sensations are, and yet they certainly come from within us.

Criticism of step 1b

It is not obvious that an unextended thing could never produce the idea of an extended thing. Descartes is relying again on the causal principle – which does not readily apply to ideas. We are clearly able to perceive representations of extended things although our minds are unextended (as Descartes claims). Perhaps we can dream them up too.

Criticism of step 2

Is everyone inclined to believe sensations come from matter? Perhaps God feeds the ideas of material things directly into our minds. This is exactly the view held by Berkeley. It could be argued this is a more efficient way of arranging things, since it produces the same effect without having all the bother of creating and maintaining a material world. Descartes rejects this possibility on the grounds that it would be a deception on God's part to make us think there is a material world, when there is not, while giving us no means to correct this view. But for Berkeley there is no deception.

Criticism: God might not exist

Descartes' proof relies on the success of his earlier proofs for God's existence – which empiricists such as Hume have attacked. If these do not succeed, then there is no guarantee that we are not being radically deceived, and the world may be very different from the way it appears.

Criticism: other ways of establishing existence of world

As we see on **pages 47–48**, empiricists such as Locke and Russell have developed their own argument for the existence of the material world.

> **Exam tip**
>
> A 25-mark question might ask you to evaluate whether Descartes produces *a priori* knowledge through his intuition and deduction thesis. Depending on the exact wording this may involve looking at the *cogito* as well as the arguments for the existence of God and of the external world. It is easy to get side-tracked when discussing these aspects, so remember to also focus on the bigger question – of whether knowledge is produced. The theme of this section is whether reason can be a source of knowledge.

Is this an a *priori* deduction?

- The argument resembles an **abduction**, but (supposedly) gives exhaustive options, so if all but one option is eliminated then the answer can be deduced. Descartes could have bypassed God and argued that the existence of the external world was the best explanation (an abduction), but this would not give him the certainty he wanted.
- The degree to which the argument is *a priori* is debatable as the whole argument is designed to explain an element of experience, namely sensation. It also draws on some *a posteriori* experience in its justification e.g. 'sensation is not subject to my will.'

Exam checklist

You should be able to:	✓
Outline and evaluate Plato's slave boy argument for innate ideas	
Outline and evaluate Leibniz's necessity of truth argument for innate ideas	
Outline and evaluate Locke's *no universal consent* argument against innate ideas	
Outline and evaluate Locke's *transparency of ideas* argument against innate ideas	
Outline and evaluate Locke's argument against innate ideas (distinguishing innate from non-innate)	
Outline and evaluate the *tabula rasa* theory	
Outline and apply *Hume's fork*	
Describe the meaning of intuition (Descartes)	
Describe the meaning of deduction (Descartes)	
Describe the meaning of clear and distinct ideas (Descartes)	
Outline and evaluate the *cogito* argument (apply Hume's fork where possible)	
Outline and evaluate the arguments for the existence of God (trademark, contingency, ontological) (apply Hume's fork where possible)	
Outline and evaluate the argument for the existence of the material world (apply Hume's fork where possible)	

Limits of knowledge

Scepticism

The differences between philosophical scepticism and normal incredulity

REVISED

Philosophical scepticism is extreme

In normal (ordinary) life, we might doubt whether it will stay dry today or whether the train will be on time. This is reasonable. In contrast, philosophers tend to doubt things that in ordinary life are very difficult, if not impossible, to doubt – for example, whether or not their hands really exist, whether other people could really be zombies with no thoughts or feelings.

Normal incredulity is sensitive to evidence

In ordinary life we doubt a claim when we think it could well be false. For example, I might doubt whether a wild mushroom is edible or not. I might use the evidence of a book and double check on the internet to overcome my doubt.

But maybe all textbooks are wrong or there is a global conspiracy of misinformation on this mushroom. We cannot check other sources as they may be involved too. These more extreme thoughts move us towards philosophical scepticism. The doubt seems immune from counter-evidence – to the point where it is almost impossible to remove.

Philosophical scepticism remains theoretical

When philosophers doubt, they may actually still hold the belief to be true. When a philosopher doubts the existence of physical objects for the sake of argument, this does not imply that she really thinks they are not real.

A philosopher will continue to lean on the very table she pretends to doubt exists. This is the reason why philosophical doubt often appears silly. The philosopher's doubts appear pointless, since they have no bearing on the practicalities of life. They also seem far-fetched, and even insane.

Purpose

Another point to make about philosophical scepticism is that it is often used to test the strength of our knowledge claims. The sceptic asks questions of the evidence supporting the knowledge claims we hold, and if we cannot provide adequate answers, the sceptic demands that we give up the claims.

By attempting to doubt such things, philosophers hope to understand what underlies our most fundamental beliefs, such as those concerning physical objects or other people. At the same time, if we can refute the sceptic, we will have vindicated our claim to know. This was what Descartes was attempting to do by using scepticism in his *Meditations*. By trying to defeat sceptical arguments, Descartes and others have tried to clarify what we can and cannot know and to establish the certainty with which we can claim knowledge.

Local and global scepticism

REVISED

Some philosophical arguments may suggest that knowledge is impossible within some particular area, perhaps knowledge of the future, of religious claims or about other minds.

Such scepticisms may be termed 'local', meaning they concern some particular and restricted domain of knowledge, but do not raise doubts about knowledge as a whole.

Other arguments, such as the idea of a brain in a vat, seem to raise doubts about all of our knowledge. These arguments conclude that knowledge in any area is impossible. Such arguments are far more radical and lead to 'universal' or 'global' scepticism, meaning they threaten to undermine the whole of our belief system.

	Normal incredulity	Philosophical scepticism
When	Happens when ordinary evidence makes us challenge a particular belief	Occurs even when ordinary evidence makes a belief very likely to be true. Often involves highly unlikely (but still possible) scenarios
Impact on behaviour	Grounded in ordinary evidence, often alters behaviour	Has a theoretical, not practical, purpose. Tends not to impact behaviour
How it spreads	Limited. Occurs against a background of other beliefs which are taken for granted	Is infectious, so tends to extend to a whole set of beliefs
Sensitivity to evidence	Sensitive to ordinary evidence. Is overcome if grounds for doubt are removed	Requires such a high burden of proof that the grounds for doubt are hard to remove
Scope	Usually directed at a particular belief – but can include a whole area, e.g. being sceptical about astrology	Can be local – restricted to sets of beliefs, e.g. religious claims. Can also be global – about knowledge in general
Purpose	Ensures a particular belief is true. Helps us guide our actions	Tests knowledge claims. Reveals hidden/basic assumptions

Descartes' three waves of doubt

REVISED

In the *Meditations*, Descartes uses his so-called **method of doubt** in an attempt to rebuild his system of belief. This involves suspending judgement about *all* the things he previously took for granted and only accepting beliefs that are **indubitable** (cannot be doubted). In this way he can achieve certainty.

He does not go through each belief individually but attempts to destroy the 'principles' or most basic beliefs, so that the rest collapse of their own accord.

Descartes employs three distinct 'waves of doubt', each more radical than the last.

Doubting the senses

Because his senses have sometimes deceived him, Descartes argues it would be best not to trust them. The possibility of perceptual error is sufficient to lead him to doubt the whole of sense experience.

> **Revision activity**
>
> Write up an example of ordinary incredulity and of philosophical scepticism. Then show how the two differ in as many ways as possible.

Criticism

We are only able to tell that our senses are sometimes deceptive precisely because on other occasions we take them to be accurate. I can only tell that a stick looks bent in water if I trust my eyes when it is not in water. In the same way, just because some paintings are forgeries, it does not follow that all paintings are forgeries – in fact, this is not possible – as forgeries can only exist if there are originals.

Response

Descartes is not saying that all his sense-based beliefs could be false, but rather that not one of them is guaranteed to be true. The key distinction here is between 'possibly all false' – all his beliefs may be false – and 'all possibly false' – some may be true, even though we may not be able to tell which.

The dreaming argument

If Descartes can have dreams which are just like being awake, then can he be sure he is not dreaming now? This possibility means that any belief drawn from what he is perceiving around him may be false.

Criticism: dreams *are* different

Dreams are very different in character from real life – we can easily tell the difference.

Descartes counters this by arguing that whatever criterion I use to tell that I am awake, it remains possible that I merely *dream* that the criterion is satisfied. So, there can never be 'any reliable way of distinguishing being awake from being asleep'.

Criticism: can't always be dreaming

The possibility of being mistaken about being awake only seems possible if sometimes we actually are awake. As with the forged painting (above), to be able to say that a dream is realistic presupposes that we are awake sometimes.

However, while such arguments might show that I am not *always* dreaming, they do not show that I am not dreaming *now*.

Criticism: 'indistinguishable' dreams?

Descartes' doubt relies on the premise that some dreams are indistinguishable from waking life. But can he know this? On the one hand, to know this premise to be true is to know such dreams to be indistinguishable. And yet if you *know* you have had such dreams, they *must* be distinguishable (otherwise you would not know you had had them).

However, Descartes does not need to *know* the premise for his doubts to work. Simply entertaining the possibility that he may have dreams which are indistinguishable from waking life may be enough to raise doubts about whether he is dreaming now.

The evil demon argument

Descartes imagines the possibility of an extremely powerful and malicious demon who employs all his energies to deceive him. Such a demon would be powerful enough to deceive him about the very existence of the physical world and also even basic operations of reasoning, such as maths.

Criticism: doubting reason is self-defeating

Can Descartes seriously doubt the possibility of rational thought itself, since he must use reason to do so? The possibility of doubt is premised on the distinction between truth and falsehood. If I can doubt something, I must know what it means to say that something may be true or false.

Criticism: empty hypothesis

Because the **evil demon**'s trickery is, *in principle*, undetectable, critics suggest it is an empty hypothesis. In most deception-based scenarios (*The Matrix*, *The Truman Show*) there is a way of discovering the deception. But if Descartes' demon is so cunning that there is no way of telling the difference between truth and deception, then for all practical purposes it makes no difference.

Imagine a counterfeit ten-pound note, which is so perfect that it cannot be spotted. No conceivable test would reveal it as a fake. If the deception is perfect, then surely it is no different from a real note. It would pass unnoticed into circulation and, the thought goes, there is no real sense in which a fake which does all that the real thing does can meaningfully be called a fake.

> **Now test yourself**
>
> Can you name Descartes' three waves of doubt? Can you articulate them accurately?
>
> TESTED

Responses to scepticism

Descartes

REVISED

Descartes uses his intuition and deduction method to try to overcome scepticism. He reaches a belief that even the demon hypothesis cannot make him doubt – *that he exists* (the *cogito*) (for issues with this, see **page 37**). From this initial belief he tries to deduce further truths that can also be free from doubt.

Descartes put the indubitable character of the *cogito* down to the fact that it can be known clearly and distinctly and concludes a general rule that whatever he perceives clearly and distinctly must be true.

Criticism

Claiming truth on the basis of an idea being clear and distinct is criticised on **page 37**. Perhaps the *cogito*'s unshakable truth lies in its self-justifying nature, not in its clarity and distinctness.

How can we be sure which ideas are clear and distinct? Even if we had exact criteria for these terms, how can we be sure we are applying them correctly? We might be deceived.

To overcome lingering doubts about whether all clear and distinct ideas can be known with certainty, Descartes attempts to prove the existence of God, as an all-good and powerful God would neither create him with such a deceptive nature nor allow him to believe with such conviction that which is actually false.

Criticism: the Cartesian circle

Descartes' proofs of God's existence have their criticisms (pages 38–40), but there is also a structural problem with Descartes' overall strategy.

Descartes needs to prove that a non-deceiving God exists to show that his clear and distinct thoughts must be true. But to establish God's existence, he has to put forward arguments using clear and distinct ideas. The approach is question begging or circular as it presupposes what it sets out to prove.

External world

Having 'proved' the existence of God, Descartes overcomes his doubts about the material world by arguing that a good God would not make his nature such as to be deceived about what is causing his perceptions of the world. They must be caused by a material reality. (For more on this see pages 40–41.)

Empiricist responses: Locke, Berkeley, Russell

REVISED

Most empiricists do not think the challenge of scepticism can be fully met. The human mind can know some things with certainty (such as relations of ideas – things true by definition), however, matters of fact (how the world is) can never be known with full certainty. But we can still have sufficiently well-founded opinions that are perfectly adequate to enable us to get on with the practical business of ordinary living.

Descartes' experience suggests that if we insist on being absolutely certain, then we may end up with very little 'knowledge'. Some empiricists argue that we should reject Descartes' infallibilism. If we are less strict about what counts as knowledge, then we can allow ourselves to know a bit more.

Locke: existence of external world

Descartes thought that the essential nature of matter was extension – which meant that its properties could be deduced via geometry. In contrast, Locke believed our knowledge is confined to the world as it appears to our senses, and we cannot penetrate through the veil of perception to reveal the essence of reality. Thus, for Locke, substance (matter) can be only be a supposition consisting of 'he knows not what'.

But that does not mean giving up on belief in the existence of the material world. The merest possibility of doubt is not a good reason for giving up on a set of beliefs. Indeed, our instincts would not let us do this.

For Locke, scepticism about the external world may be possible at a theoretical level but not at the practical level. Since the practical business of living is what really matters to us, we should be content with this. A sceptical scenario may be logically possible, but this does not imply that we cannot be as sure as we need to be that it does not obtain.

Russell

Like Locke, Russell recognised that we cannot demonstrate conclusively the existence of the material world, but noted that we cannot demonstrate conclusively that it does *not* exist either. We are presented with a choice – to accept that the physical world does exist or that it does not. For Russell, the physical world hypothesis is by far the best option. (This is an abduction – an inference to the best explanation.)

The existence of a physical world can explain why our sense experience behaves in regular and predictable ways. For example, an apple lying forgotten in a drawer will appear shrivelled and rotten when discovered months later. This is because the apple physically exists and has undergone a transformation while not being observed.

In the alternative hypothesis (there is no mind-independent physical object), the apple itself provides no explanation for my experience. The whole experience would be a complete mystery. It follows that it is reasonable to suppose that there is a physical world.

Berkeley

Most scepticism thrives because of the gap between our perception and reality. This gap allows for dreams, errors or demons to be the possible cause of the perception.

In Berkeley's idealist view of perception, there is no gap between the perception and the object. There is no mind-independent reality. To be is to be perceived. By denying that matter exists, Berkeley can assert that we have secure knowledge of reality precisely because that reality is within the mind, so that we are directly aware of it.

If physical objects are no more than what they appear to be, then there is nothing that is hidden from our view – no gap between perceiver and perceived – and so no room for sceptical arguments to gain purchase (see more on **page 23**).

Reliabilism

REVISED

Reliabilism claims that knowledge is reliably produced true belief. A person can have knowledge even if they cannot give a 'justification' for the belief. So, if you can reliably tell a pair of twins apart, then it does not matter if you cannot say how you do it. As long as you can reliably do this, then you know which twin is which.

Sceptical arguments often exploit weaknesses in the justification of knowledge. You see a red car and believe there is a red car in the road. But what is your justification? Your eyesight? But eyes can be deceiving. By attacking the justification, the claim to knowledge is undermined. However, reliabilism denies that we need a justification for our beliefs, so the sceptical argument does not get off the ground. If the belief is reliably produced, then you know there is a car there. Beliefs can count as knowledge even if we are unable to provide a cogent defence of our belief.

But what of the kind of global scepticism presented by the brain in a vat (BIV)-type scenarios? Here standard definitions of knowledge involving justification can falter. Internal justifications such as 'I know there is a red car because I saw it' break down under scrutiny. The key difficulty is that

> ### Now test yourself
> Summarise the 'empiricist' responses to scepticism from Locke, Russell and Berkeley. What sorts of argument do they use?
> TESTED

your justification – 'I saw it' – would be the same if you were in the BIV world or the normal word. And as you do not know which world you are in, then your justification fails, and you cannot know the red car is there (or even know that the world exists).

However, as far as reliabilism is concerned, although I cannot tell whether or not I am a brain in a vat, this does not show that I do not have knowledge of the world. For if I am in the normal world, then my beliefs about the physical world are produced by a reliable process, and so count as knowledge. I do not additionally have to justify or prove that I am *not* a brain in a vat. Further, if I do have knowledge, and know that there is a red car in the road, then it must be the case that the material world exists.

I may not have a reliable way of knowing whether I am a brain in a vat or not, so I cannot necessarily know *that* I have knowledge. But this is not important. As no internal justification for knowledge is needed, I do not have to show that I know that I know, in order to actually have knowledge. It is enough that my beliefs are reliably produced for me to have knowledge.

So reliabilism shows that we can have knowledge of the world, despite global scepticism. However, we may not be able to know that we have knowledge.

Criticism

Reliabilism shows how we can still have knowledge despite the existence of brain in a vat scenarios. However, this has also been used as a criticism of the theory. If my belief I am holding a pen is justified in the real world, then, given that the experience is exactly the same, it seems right to say that the belief I am holding a pen would also be justified in a brain in a vat scenario (it just wouldn't be true). In replacing the concept of 'justification' with 'reliably produced', reliabilism can account for our (lack of) knowledge in brain in a vat scenarios but, in doing so, it does not seem to give an adequate account of the relationship between our beliefs and our justifications.

Exam checklist

You should be able to:	✓
Describe the nature and purpose of philosophical scepticism	
Compare and distinguish between normal incredulity and philosophical scepticism	
Describe the differences between local and global scepticism and the global application of philosophical scepticism	
Critically discuss Descartes' three waves of doubt	
Evaluate Descartes' response to doubt	
Evaluate the empiricists' response to doubt (Locke, Russell, Berkeley)	
Evaluate reliabilism as a response to doubt	

How should I behave? What is **right** and wrong? **Ethics** is the branch of philosophy that explores this arena. The word *morality* is sometimes used instead of *ethics*.

Normative theories

Three levels of ethical discussion

Traditionally, **moral philosophy** is divided into three areas and this section explores all three.

One area, **normative ethics**, explores what makes for morally **good** and bad behaviour in general. What are the underlying reasons why we might call an action a good one?

A second area applies the answers from the first area to very specific dilemmas. This area is known as **applied ethics**.

A third area, **meta-ethics**, takes a step back from the discussions above and, instead, focuses the attention on moral discussion itself, asking questions such as: *Is morality a human construction? Do moral words have meanings?*

Figure 2.1 **The three levels of ethics.** (A) Meta-ethics asks questions about morality itself. (B) Normative ethics seeks to answer questions about good and bad in general. (C) Applied ethics works out how to apply the answer from (B) to specific cases.

Comparison of the three normative ethical theories

This section outlines and compares the three main normative theories of ethics:
- **utilitarianism** (which emphasises the consequences of any action)
- **Kantian ethics** (which emphasises the motive for actions)
- **virtue ethics** (which focuses on the **person** who acts on the world).

The meaning of good, bad, right, wrong within each of the three approaches

Utilitarians focus on what's Good, Kantians focus on what's Right, virtue ethicists focus on good character (virtue).

	Utilitarian ethics	Kantian ethics	Virtue ethics
Good	= an action which maximises happiness/utility and minimises pain		= a person who is virtuous (their character consists of very many virtues)
Bad	= an action which leads to more pain than pleasure/utility		= a person who is vicious (their character consists of many flaws and vices)
Right		= an action which is in accordance with what duty demands	
Wrong		= an action which is against what duty demands	
	Act-centred theories		Agent-centred theories

Similarities and differences across the three approaches

Here are two ways of illustrating the differences and similarities – a table, and a set of venn diagrams.

	Utilitarian ethics	Kantian ethics	Virtue ethics
Focus is on actions	Yes	Yes	No
Focus is on agents	No	No	Yes
Asks 'what would happen if everyone behaved like that?'	Yes – rule utilitarians at least	Yes	No
Reason is important	No	Yes	Yes (equal with feelings)
Feelings are important	Yes (pleasure and pain)	No	Yes (equal with reason)
Considers long-term implications	Yes	Not really	Yes (in terms of effect on character)
Considers self more than other people	No	No	Yes
Considers other people more than self	Yes	Yes	No
Morality conflicts with self-interest	Sometimes	Yes	No (see page 90)
What matters are the outcomes of an action	Yes	No	Yes (lots of virtues are bound up with positive outcomes)
What matters are the motives for an action	No	Yes	Yes (a virtue is only a genuine virtue if it is the result of the correct motive)
	Act-centred theories		Agent-centred theories

Note that Kantian and Utilitarian theories seem to be opposites (one judges the motives before an action, the other judges the consequences after an action), but Julia Annas identifies them both as act-centred theories, in contrast to agent-centred virtue ethics.

Is the theory act-centred or agent-centred?

Utilitarian ethics / Kantian ethics — *Act-centred*

Virtue ethics — *Agent-centred*

Does the theory focus on reason or feelings?

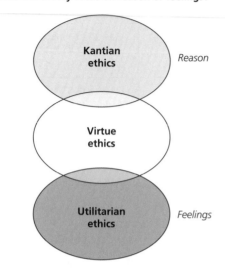

Kantian ethics — *Reason*

Virtue ethics

Utilitarian ethics — *Feelings*

Does the theory focus on outcomes or motives?

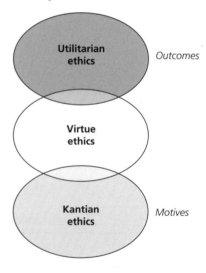

Utilitarian ethics — *Outcomes*

Virtue ethics

Kantian ethics — *Motives*

Does the theory focus on self-interest or the interests of others?

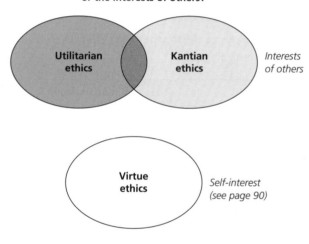

Utilitarian ethics / Kantian ethics — *Interests of others*

Virtue ethics — *Self-interest (see page 90)*

Does the theory have a formula to help apply it to real life situations?

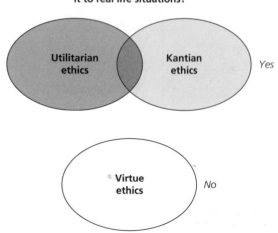

Utilitarian ethics / Kantian ethics — *Yes*

Virtue ethics — *No*

What is the time over which judgements are made?

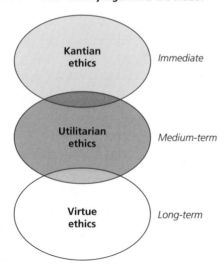

Kantian ethics — *Immediate*

Utilitarian ethics — *Medium-term*

Virtue ethics — *Long-term*

Now test yourself answers at **www.hoddereducation.co.uk/myrevisionnotesdownloads**

Utilitarianism

Utility and maximising utility

The word utilitarianism is derived from the concept of **utility** or usefulness. Any object or action has utility (is useful) if it helps achieve a specific goal (or goals).

Hedonistic utilitarianism

Bentham argued that the ultimate goal of all actions is gaining/pleasure and avoiding pain. As such, an object or action has utility if it brings pleasure/avoids pain.

Two theories related to pleasure are:

1 *Psychological hedonism.* A **descriptive** theory (not a moral one) of human motivation. It claims that the individual's potential pleasure and avoidance of pain are the sole aims of the individual's action.
2 *Classic (or hedonistic) utilitarianism.* A moral theory that claims that a right action is one that maximises general happiness/minimises pain (not just the individual's).

Bentham draws on both theories in this famous quote:

> Nature has placed mankind under the governance of two sovereign masters, pain and pleasure. It is for them alone to point out what we ought to do, as well as to determine what we shall do. On the one hand the standard of right and wrong, on the other the chain of causes and effects are fastened to their throne.
>
> Bentham, *Principles* p. 1

Bentham's utility calculus (act utilitarianism and rule utilitarianism)

Act utilitarianism

The moral value of any act is calculated by considering its consequences (which makes it a **consequentialist ethical theory**). To calculate the moral worth, add up all the pleasure the act brings and subtract all the pain/suffering. An action is good if it brings about more pleasure than pain (perfectionists say a good act is the one that brings the most pleasure, not just some).

Consider a mugging. The mugger gains a phone, which brings short-term pleasure. However, the victim will suffer greatly and over a longer period. Plus, the victim's family and friends will be distressed. The mugging causes a lot of suffering, so is a bad act.

Bentham conceived a (somewhat hypothetical) 'utility calculus' to help calculate moral worth. This involves taking into account aspects of pleasure such as the intensity, duration, certainty, remoteness, fecundity, purity and extent.

Rule utilitarianism

Critics of act utilitarianism argue the theory is impractical.
- Long-term consequences can never be known.
- It takes too long to calculate the moral worth.
- The theory leads to counter-intuitive results (for example, killing and harvesting the organs from an innocent person to save multiple people).

Rule utilitarianism overcomes these issues. It argues that you should follow general rules (or what Mill calls secondary principles) such as 'don't kill' and 'don't steal'. In this theory an act is good if it follows a suitable rule and a rule is good if it is one that will increase happiness.

Criticism

Rule utilitarianism collapses into act utilitarianism. Most basic rules are too general and have legitimate exceptions. 'Don't lie' is a rule, but 'Do not lie, unless to a potential murderer' is a better one. 'Do not lie unless to potential murderers, or to partners when they ask if you like their new haircuts' is a better one still. Every time there is a set of cases where lying may produce more happiness, we could make another amendment. Smart argues that, taken to its logical conclusion, this would end up with a version of act utilitarianism, but with rules that apply to very specific sets of circumstances.

> **Revision activity**
>
> A five-mark question might ask you to outline act or rule utilitarianism. Practise writing short, accurate accounts of each version.

John Stuart Mill's qualitative hedonistic utilitarianism

REVISED

In Bentham's time, overcrowding in London had led to the poor living very difficult lives. Many sought comfort in drinking gin. Critics of utilitarianism claimed the theory advocated the pursuit of mindless drinking as a morally good thing to do (as it gave pleasure).

Higher and lower pleasures

Mill defended the theory, in part by introducing a new distinction between 'higher' and 'lower' pleasures. Mill thought that pleasures of the mind were superior to physical pleasures as they were likely to last longer and so give more pleasure, but he also claimed that the 'quantity only' approach was not needed.

Mill argued that many humans would prefer the pleasures of the mind (higher pleasures) over those of the body (lower pleasures), *even if* the pleasures of the body were more pleasurable.

> It is better to be a human being dissatisfied than a pig satisfied; better to be Socrates dissatisfied than a fool satisfied. And if the fool, or the pig, are of a different opinion, it is because they only know their own side of the question. The other party to the comparison knows both sides.
>
> Mill, *Utilitarianism* p.7

Mill suggested that some pleasures are inherently better than others. Someone who has experienced both would value higher pleasures more, even though sometimes they may be less pleasant.

Only those who can appreciate both types of pleasure are able to say which is the better. Mill termed these people 'competent judges'. A pig cannot say whether reading Shakespeare is valuable or not.

Criticism

Is this hedonistic utilitarianism anymore? Mill's distinction means that some pleasures can be 'better' even if they give less pleasure. Does this make sense from a hedonistic utilitarian? It would seem that if something could be less *pleasant*, yet *better*, then we are no longer seeking to maximise *pleasure*.

Defence: Mill may be claiming that higher and lower pleasures are simply incommensurable – rather than one being less pleasant than the other. For example, blue is different from red. No amount of blue will be the same as any amount of red; they are simply different.

Mill claims that even for lower pleasures/pains, we cannot really compare two side by side; we can only ask someone who has experienced both (a competent judge) which is the better or worse.

Also, Mill did not see happiness just as a question of pleasure. Humans have the capacity to reason and develop. In his earlier work, *On Liberty*, Mill gave a different account of utility which reflects this broader, developmental view of human happiness.

Criticism: loses simplicity

What makes utilitarianism so appealing is its simplicity. We can calculate what action to take by weighing up the quantities of pleasure (and pain) involved. Once Mill introduces the notion of quality into the discussion, then some of the simplicity disappears. Imagine a council is trying to decide whether to build a gym or a library. Is a library (higher pleasure) infinitely better than a gym (lower pleasure)? Does one library = ten gyms?

Criticism: elitism

This is cultural elitism. Some have argued that the term 'higher pleasures' just means 'the things that Mill and his friends like to do' and is snobbishly dismissive of the pleasures of the masses.

Mill's 'proof' of the greatest happiness principle

REVISED

Mill claimed that the ultimate principles of morality, like all first principles, cannot be proven, but reasons/facts can be given for believing these principles. His 'proof' looks like this:

1 The only evidence that something is visible is that it can actually be seen.
2 Similarly, the only evidence that something is desirable is that it is actually desired.
3 Each person desires their own happiness.
4 Therefore *each person's happiness is desirable.*
5 The general happiness is desirable.
6 Each person's happiness is a good to that person.
7 The general happiness is a good to the aggregate of all persons.
8 Happiness is the only good.

Criticism: equivocation

Mill suggests the property of being 'desirable' is like the property of being 'visible'. However, it can be argued that desirability is crucially different as it has two meanings.

Sense 1: A factual sense, meaning *that which is able to be desired* (which could be anything – even morally questionable things).

Sense 2: A more moral sense, meaning *that which ought to be desired.*

These two meanings can be seen by considering that not everything that is desired (in sense 1) is desirable (in sense 2). We can think of all manner of gross things that people desire, but which we wouldn't call 'desirable'. Historically, owning slaves has been desired by many people, but is not desirable!

The charge is that Mill is using 'desired' in sense 1 (people do desire happiness) to suggest happiness is morally 'desirable' in sense 2. He is guilty of equivocation (using a term with more than one meaning misleadingly).

In Mill's defence, he is not trying to deduce that happiness is worthy of desire. But how else are we to decide what is desirable, if not by looking at what is desired? Mill is an empiricist, so believes that only experience is capable of telling us what is desirable.

Criticism: fallacy of the composition

If each person wants their own happiness, it does not follow that each of us also wants the general happiness. This is known as the **fallacy** of composition. For example, each person might want to win the National Lottery, but each person does not want everyone to win the lottery this week.

Criticism: mystical being

Mill claims general happiness is desirable to the aggregate of people. But the aggregate of people is not the sort of thing that has desires. In Mill's defence, he may not be claiming that the mystical 'aggregate' desires the general good. Rather, if each of us thinks of happiness as a good, then from an *impartial* point of view, overall general happiness is the good.

Criticism: the is–ought gap

See **page 100** and the naturalistic fallacy (**page 97**).

Mill's proof continued: happiness as the ultimate end

In the final part of the 'proof', Mill acknowledges that people do desire other things (**virtue**, money etc.) as ends in themselves (not just as a means to happiness). This is because these things are part of what happiness means to that person (they are constitutive of happiness). But this only happens over time. For a baby, money is just a kind of funny paper. It is only through culture and socialisation that we come to see money initially as a means to happiness, and then, as a constituent part of this happiness. As such, we should see happiness as the ultimate end.

Non-hedonistic utilitarianism

Hedonistic/classic utilitarians aim to maximise happiness. Other forms of utilitarianism share the idea that we should maximise something, but argue this is not just pleasure. For this reason, they are termed non-hedonistic forms of utilitarianism, the most famous of which is preference utilitarianism.

Preference utilitarianism

Preference utilitarianism suggests an action should be judged by how it conforms to the preferences of all those affected by the action (and its consequences). A good act is one which maximises the satisfaction of the preferences of all those involved.

> **Now test yourself**
>
> Outline the key stages of Mill's proof of utilitarianism and provide three criticisms.
>
> TESTED
>
> REVISED

So, when considering whether to turn off the life-support machine of someone terminally ill, rather than aiming to maximise happiness, we should find out what all the relevant parties would prefer and maximise their preferences.

Many decisions will be the same whichever form of utilitarianism we choose, but the reasons may be different. Classic utilitarians may claim that lying is wrong as it often leads to *unhappiness*. For a preference utilitarian, lying is also often wrong, but this is because it goes against the *preference* we have to know the truth.

Advantages

The focus on pleasure at the core of utilitarianism can be counter-intuitive. The gruesome killings in the Colosseum entertained thousands — but surely were not a good thing. Stand-up comedians bring huge pleasure, yet few would claim that their work has the same moral value as that of doctors volunteering in a war zone.

Preference utilitarianism provides a solution. Most people's preference to be pain-free is far, far stronger than their preference for gaining pleasure. This is why it is morally better to help those suffering than it is to make non-suffering people happier. The rise in happiness levels of both might be the same, but the strength of preference is definitely on the side of the sufferer. This is why our moral priorities should be to relieve pain and suffering in the world.

Preference utilitarianism also has an advantage in that preferences are easier to find out — we can ask people.

Criticism: bad preferences

Surely we should not maximise bad/crazy preferences? Imagine David has become increasingly psychotic and wants to punch strangers. Is it right to help him?

- First, other people's preference not to be punched would be much stronger than David's desire to punch, so it would be wrong to help.
- Second, because David's mental health is an issue, we should consider what his preferences might be after a suitable course of therapy. Punching people is David's manifest desire, but it is not his true desire.

Preference utilitarians try to imagine an 'ideal viewpoint' position — they imagine the desires from the perspective that the person was well and had all the relevant knowledge.

Criticism: weighing up preferences

Bentham's hedonistic calculus attempted to quantify different pleasures to help moral decision-making. Preference utilitarianism needs something equivalent to this. Imagine some people are for, and some against, building a proposed airport, then what is the morally right thing to do? Is it a question of numbers, or does strength of preference make a difference? Also, what about the preferences of people who are not directly affected by the airport, or even the expressed preferences of the dead — should these all count?

Exam tip

When considering the four issues (stealing, simulated killing, eating animals, telling lies), the reasoning that follows from preference utilitarianism is different from act and rule utilitarianism — especially on the issues of eating meat and telling lies. Make sure to include the preference utilitarian angle if exploring an issue from the perspective of utilitarianism.

Issues with utilitarianism

Is pleasure the only good?

REVISED

The idea that pleasure is the ultimate end of our actions is a simple idea, although some argue it paints an unpleasant view of the human condition – that of pleasure-seeking animals with brains acting as a sort of computer to calculate maximum pleasure.

Some religious believers have claimed that seeking pleasure is not good, but is actually wrong. Instead, these people have chosen to avoid pleasure and some religious sects even used self-chastisement (whipping oneself) as part of this philosophy of avoiding pleasure.

However, Bentham claims that even these people are still driven by pleasure and pain – perhaps by the prospect of pleasure in the next life, or the avoidance of pain through the punishment of God.

Nozick's pleasure machine

(This is adapted from the philosopher Nozick.) Imagine scientists have developed an amazing new pleasure machine. You enter and are plugged into a hyper-real virtual-reality machine. You are guaranteed to live a pleasurable life – maybe win an Oscar or become a top footballer. Your memory will be tinkered with, so that you will not even know that you are in a machine.

The only downside is that once you have stepped into the machine, you cannot come out. You will live a long and healthy life of guaranteed pleasurable sensations. Would you plug yourself in for the rest of your life?

If you are happy to sign up to the machine, then this seems to prove the truth of psychological **hedonism**. However, if you are not ready to sign up, perhaps psychological hedonism is wrong? Perhaps pleasure is not your only goal?

Criticism 1: it is not *pleasure* that we seek, but things outside of our heads

Nozick created the thought experiment to show that the idea of humans just seeking things inside our heads (pleasure) may be wrong. What people often want are specific states of affairs in the world. They want their children to be happy or for people to think well of them. People want these relationships and states of affairs in the world, and not just for the sensations that might then result in their heads. Many would refuse the machine, as what they seek are things in a real world, not sensations.

Criticism 2: (related to 1) it is not *pleasure* that we seek, but specific things

Imagine you have been collecting Hello Kitty stickers. You *really* want the final missing sticker. Bentham would claim that the sticker is just a means to gaining pleasure. However, you may feel strongly that what you actually want is the sticker, not the pleasure it will bring. If I offered to give you the equivalent amount of pleasure, but from another source, you may still claim it is the sticker you want, not just a quantity of pleasure. People have died fighting against injustices, to gain the right to vote etc. Very few people would put their life on the line just for more 'pleasure'.

> **Revision activity**
>
> Can you see how criticising the idea of pleasure as the only good can lead someone towards preference utilitarianism?

Fairness and individual liberty/rights

Act utilitarianism can lead to some counter-intuitive moral **judgements** – for example, it may be good to sacrifice an innocent scapegoat to placate the masses.

Imagine a rich family kidnap an orphan boy from a poor country and keep him as their slave. The boy is well-fed, not beaten and his work greatly increases the happiness of the family. The kidnapping seems to maximise overall happiness. But is this right?

Rule utilitarianism can avoid these odd conclusions by arguing that following rules/ideals such as the right to life, **liberty** and freedom of speech is the best way to maximise happiness. But utilitarians do *not* recognise these ideals as having moral worth in themselves. They are merely useful devices which help bring about overall happiness.

Criticism

Critics object, claiming that ideals such as liberty, honour and justice have value as ends in themselves. They are morally primitive and do not derive their moral worth from their ability to maximise happiness. The case of the kidnapping is wrong because it denies the boy his liberty. Liberty and fairness, and so on, are worth pursuing as ends in themselves – independently of whether or not they maximise happiness.

Indeed, people have undergone great hardships, including sacrificing their own lives in the name of liberty, democracy and justice. It *could* be argued that these people were just trying to maximise happiness, but do people really sacrifice their lives for the ideal of maximising happiness?

Mill on liberty: the risk of the 'tyranny of the majority'

If you were reluctant to step into the pleasure machine (**page 58**), it could be because you did not like the idea of being trapped inside. Perhaps you valued your liberty more than your happiness. Mill was a passionate advocate for liberty.

Mill noted how history is littered with examples of unelected leaders tyrannising the masses. But this problem did not end with the arrival of democracy.

Although considered 'the will of the people', in theory, and practice, democracy is only the will of the majority. There is potential for the majority to oppress others – the so-called 'tyranny of the majority' (a phrase popularised by Mill, though it pre-dated him). This oppression could be through direct legislation or through the sheer weight of social opinion making it difficult for minorities to exercise identities/freedom.

Mill argued that the *only* reason governments and other individuals should interfere in our lives is to prevent us causing harm to others (this is known as Mill's *harm principle*). As long as what we are doing does not harm others, then individuals should be left to pursue their own lives in the ways they see fit.

His account of liberty has been hugely influential. Mill claimed it is consistent with the principle of utility – that is, adopting a 'hands-off' approach will lead to more happiness in the long run. However, many dispute whether this is the case and would claim that liberty is an end in its own right.

> **Revision activity**
>
> Provide a short, accurate account of what Mill meant by the phrase 'tyranny of the majority'.

Problems with calculating utility

Average or total happiness

Should we aim for average or total happiness? This is a real question for governments. Is it better to have large populations who are less happy (perhaps because of overcrowding)? If so, providing free contraception might be morally wrong. Or smaller populations who may be happier per person, but with a lower total happiness? Then providing free contraception may be the right thing to do.

Distribution of happiness

According to utilitarianism, everyone's happiness counts equally. We all count for one. Nevertheless, most actions only affect some people. This raises some difficult questions in our deliberation. Is it better to make one person 50 points happier or five people 10 points happier? The total happiness is the same in both cases. Left-leaning thinkers argue that a wider, more even distribution is the ideal at which to aim.

Do consequences end?

You save a drowning boy, who in later life becomes a dictator responsible for the deaths of millions. Is your action good or bad? The problem is that if the moral worth of an act is based on its consequences, then it has to be constantly revised and no 'final' moral value can be assigned.

Saving the boy would always be a praiseworthy act, as you could not reasonably foresee the longer-term consequences. The problem lies in deciding the moral worth of an act – was it good or bad?

Whose happiness? Humans or animals?

The basis for moral equality is our sentience, our common ability to feel pain and pleasure. Peter Singer argues that as animals are also sentient, we should also take their interests into account. To not do so would be an example of speciesism (treating species differently for no good reason).

Singer's argument (from *marginal cases*) might be summarised as follows:

P1 If only humans have moral status, there must be some special quality that all humans share.

P2 All human-specific possibilities for such a quality will be a quality that some humans lack (for example, intelligence).

P3 The only possible candidates will be qualities that other animals have too.

C Therefore, we cannot argue that only human beings deserve moral status.

Criticism: an alien way of discussing animals

Cora Diamond objects to Singer's approach of 'lining up' all beings and judging their moral worth based only on sentience. If sentience were the only factor, then we should have no problem in eating dead humans or amputated limbs.

Yet this *is* a problem. To understand why we have to engage with the complexity of our attitudes to animals and humans.

Animals can be pets, pests, meat, vermin, predators, cute and so on. Likewise, humans can be friends, lovers, enemies, slaves etc. Diamond argues that to change people's views, we have to argue from within this complex existing moral landscape, not just rank everything by sentience.

Cora analyses a moment in the Spanish Civil War when Orwell found himself unable to shoot a half-dressed man running away holding up his trousers. 'I had come here to shoot at "Fascists", but a man who is holding up his trousers is not a "Fascist", he is visibly a fellow-creature, similar to yourself, and you do not feel like shooting at him'.

Orwell sees fellowship in the enemy and is unable to shoot. Similar moments of realisation may occur in relation to animals. Someone may suddenly see not just a sheep, but a fellow creature, and can no longer stomach a lamb casserole. It is in these moments that vegetarians are made – from within our complex conceptual understanding and not in the application of abstract, alien concepts.

Defenders of Singer's approach might argue that philosophy is *precisely* the attempt to define concepts and apply abstract ideas to clarify our thinking.

> **Revision activity**
>
> Diamond's approach to ethics is one that avoids narrow 'systems' but instead embraces the complexity of our existing moral views. This can make her criticisms of utilitarianism hard to articulate. Practise writing out her criticisms then think of a way to memorise your account.

Issues around partiality

REVISED

Bentham was passionate about equality, especially for women. He saw everyone as equally important: 'every individual in the country tells for one; no individual for more than one'.

Bentham was writing primarily for governments, and most of us would want our government to treat each citizen's welfare and happiness as having equal worth. But does this also apply to individuals making moral decisions? Should a good utilitarian treat all people equally in their actions?

If so, this seems to imply that we should never be partial – that is, to favour ourselves, or those close to us, when making moral decisions. This makes our moral duties far-reaching. Given that there are starving people in the world, it seems that we should give nearly all our money to help these people – and should do this every time we get money.

Are we really obliged to treat people we've never met equally with family and friends? Imagine this scenario. Your house is burning. You rush inside to help and find two people lying unconscious. You can only carry one out. One is a brilliant scientist who is working on a cure for cancer; the other is your son. Who should you save?

Act utilitarianism and rule utilitarianism

An act utilitarian may say that saving the scientist is more likely to maximise general happiness. It is the right thing to do. It may be understandable to want to save your son, but it would be morally wrong. We may have instincts to protect family, but we should use reason to transcend these.

However, most people would save their own son. It can be argued that this is the right thing to do, because we have moral obligations to our family and friends. In other words, we have a moral **duty** to be partial, not impartial, in some circumstances. Looking after families and caring for people we love has moral worth in itself and should not be trumped by the need to maximise general happiness. Utilitarianism is counter-intuitive in this regard.

A rule utilitarian might claim that saving your son is the right thing to do, as the rule of looking after family is a good one (it ensures that everyone is looked after, and this will maximise happiness). Furthermore, requiring everyone to be perfectly impartial would lower general happiness. Having family and friends that we care for is an integral part of our happiness – giving this up would make us all unhappy. So, the rule of **partiality** is a good one. (As long as this does not impact on the **rights** of others, as these also make us happy. So, nepotism – giving favourable treatment to family in the workplace etc. – would be a bad thing.)

How impartial should governments be?

We want governments to be impartial to their citizens, but what about the broader world? Should we give more tax money to overseas aid to help others?

A rule utilitarian may argue that the best overall rule is that every country looks after its own population (after all, the UK government's money comes from UK taxpayers). Others think this is unfair and that rich countries should not sit back and watch fellow humans starve and suffer.

Even within this country, should all people's happiness be treated equally? For example, some people feel it unfair that recently arrived refugees get some form of access to housing (often very limited) when they themselves have found it very difficult to gain social housing. Should the government take everyone's welfare into account equally? Or should those who have lived here 'longer' have priority?

Moral integrity and intentions of the individual
REVISED

Bernard Williams argued that ethical systems such as utilitarianism (and Kantian ethics) may require us to do things that challenge our sense of personal/moral integrity.

Imagine the following scenario (adapted from Williams). A botanist, Jim, is working in a lawless country and ends up in a small town, where the local warlord treats him as a guest of honour. The warlord has recently kidnapped twenty people and plans to kill them. The warlord says that if Jim personally shoots one of them, he will release the others as a sign of goodwill. If Jim does not do this, he will kill them all. What should Jim do?

An act utilitarian would say there is no dilemma here. You kill the one to save the nineteen. However, Jim does not want to harm, let alone kill, anyone. It goes against one of his key principles. He has lived his life around this principle and it defines, in part, who he is. If Jim did shoot one person, then his sense of self and sense of purpose may be destroyed.

The problem is that utilitarianism doesn't allow you to draw a line in the sand and say, *I will not do that.* Yet Williams argues, for many people, their personal integrity demands that there are such lines in the sand. The character of the person committing the act may not reckon in the moral value of the act, but it does matter to the person committing the act.

Put formally, William's argument might be summarised as follows:
P1 Personal integrity requires there are things (X) that you would not do.
P2 Using a utilitarian framework, a scenario can always be created whereby X is the right thing to do.
C   Therefore utilitarianism undermines our personal integrity.

> **Exam tip**
>
> Remember that William's criticism that utilitarianism can undermine our moral integrity can also apply to Kantian ethics. Any 'system' of morality may require actions that go against your own personal values. It is a good criticism to revise.

In defence you could argue that a person's sense of moral/personal integrity is culturally acquired. If we cede to our intuitions or personal integrity, this gives too much weight to a person's upbringing, which in turn can act to maintain the moral status quo, which is not always good.

Intentions

In judging an act as good or bad, utilitarianism focuses solely on the consequences. This has advantages as consequences are easier to identify than motives. However, a big problem for utilitarianism is that ignoring the intentions can feel counter-intuitive.

Simra visits her elderly grandma once a week. She buys a few groceries, tidies up a little, helps Grandma with her post and reads to her. Grandma loves the visits; Simra less so, but she goes out of a sense of duty. Maisie also visits her elderly grandma once a week and just like Simra, buys groceries, tidies up etc. However, Maisie visits to increase the chances of getting money in Grandma's will.

Which of these two almost identical acts has the most moral worth? Many would argue that Simra's does. But the pleasure that each of the acts brings is roughly the same, so for a utilitarian both acts are equally good. However, this feels counter-intuitive. Surely the motive for carrying out the act plays a part in its moral worth? A utilitarian would disagree. They would claim that the acts have the same moral worth.

In defence, utilitarians use the concepts of blame and praise, as distinct to the moral worth of the action. In this way, the intention of the **agent** can be acknowledged in our moral language. Also, our moral assessment of people can be based on their intentions. So Maisie's act is good, but not praiseworthy (as cynical self-centred acts tend to cause suffering).

Applied ethics: utilitarianism

Stealing

REVISED

For an act utilitarian, stealing would be morally good if the happiness gained from the theft outweighs the pain caused. For an act utilitarian, the end (happiness) can justify the means, even when the 'means' is illegal.

But in general, theft is wrong, as the pain caused to the victim far outweighs the pleasure gained by the thief. Also stealing is usually illegal and people get upset when others break the law, so this adds to the total pain caused.

Having laws around property ownership makes us all feel more secure, and this lawfulness is a big source of background happiness. Because of the strong disapproval of law-breaking, the default position of an act utilitarian is that law-breaking is morally wrong. As stealing is illegal, if you are caught, you may well be punished, and this too adds to the pain in the world.

What about secretly stealing from a billionaire to help the poor? An act utilitarian might say this is a good act as it adds happiness to the world. However, oddly, were the thief to be caught, it would become a bad act, as the money might be reclaimed and the victim and the criminal will suffer. The moral worth of the act seems to depend on the thief getting away with it.

For many people, this is counter-intuitive: what makes illegal acts bad is committing the act itself, not the consequences. It is just bad to break the law. This is close to the position of strong rule utilitarianism: it is always wrong to break a rule/law (as long as the law is one that overall maximises happiness), as the moral value of an act comes from its observance of the rule.

A subtler version of the rule may be in general do not steal, but there may be some occasions when stealing saves lives and then it is okay.

Simulated killing

Does being entertained by simulated death produce more happiness than it does harm? Could alternatives be produced that are more pleasurable, with less harm caused? Would the world be happier without simulated death, or with it?

According to utilitarianism, such entertainments are not intrinsically wrong, as wrong is defined entirely by ends (pain or less happiness), not the means.

On the positive side (happiness):
● These entertainments produce a lot of pleasure. They are very popular.
● There are often secondary pleasures gained from engaging with a part of a specific culture – chatting with friends about games, conventions and so on.
● They are also part of successful industries that supply jobs, create wealth and advance technology.
● Video games can have beneficial effects in terms of motor skills.
● In the last twenty years, violent crime has decreased in the UK, whilst violent video games and films have boomed. This suggests that any causal link between video games and violence cannot be strong.

On the negative/harm side:
● Violent films, and in particular games, have been linked to increased antisocial behaviour in the short and longer terms (however, there is also evidence that shows there is very little link).
● Too much time spent watching/playing can have harmful effects on health (in terms of sedentary lifestyle).
● People disapprove of these activities and this causes some sadness.

Higher/lower distinction

For Mill, such entertainments may be classed as lower pleasures, which, though still good, are of lower worth. Mill wanted utility not just to be about physical pleasure but:

> utility in the largest sense, grounded on the permanent interests of man as a progressive being.

Mill, On Liberty, p.7

Mill may argue that such pleasures appeal to our baser, animal side and not to our progressive, intellectual side. Holding a higher/lower qualitative distinction may alter the result of the utilitarian calculus.

Liberty

Mill also argued passionately that the secondary principle (or rule) of liberty should play a central role in utilitarianism. We should all be free to pursue our own pleasures, as long as we do not harm others. This maximises happiness in the long term. Exceptions to the principle of liberty are made in the cases of children, where parent/state should act in the best interest of the child.

Eating animals

Many humans gain pleasure from eating animals, which would seem to suggest that it may be a good thing – though the environmental impact needs to be considered too as a long-term consequence.

Previously we saw Singer (**page 60**) argue that the pain and pleasure of animals has moral weight – so we need to take this into account too. Despite this, he claims that eating meat is not always wrong.

Singer is/was a preference utilitarian. What makes killing humans morally wrong is not specifically the potential loss of pleasure, but that the killing goes against the preference of the victim (and the victim's family and friends). Staying alive is (generally) the strongest preference that anyone has.

Also, in killing someone, we are not merely overriding one of their preferences (to stay alive), but also their preference to learn Spanish, learn to make bread, watch all of the *Avenger* movies and so on. We are going against thousands of their wishes and desires.

Can we say the same about animals? They are not likely to have a range of conscious preferences (with the possible exception of great apes). We can infer from their behaviour that animals prefer not to be in pain, but can we even say that an animal has a conscious preference to stay alive? Probably not, as the animal lacks the necessary conceptual framework. In which case, the painless killing of say, a sheep, does not go against its preference, so is not morally wrong on this account. Also, if the sheep was replaced by a lamb then the total amount of sheep pleasure in the world remains the same.

However, Singer claims that most current forms of farming cause suffering to animals, so it would be wrong to eat meat if we could gain our food in other ways. But, in theory, there could be farms that treat animals well and slaughter them painlessly, in which case there may be nothing morally wrong with eating the animals.

Now test yourself

Outline Singer's argument(s) for why animal suffering is morally relevant. Can you also articulate why it might be acceptable to eat meat as a preference utilitarian?

TESTED

Telling lies

For an act utilitarian, the end justifies the means so lying is morally acceptable if it maximises happiness/minimises harm. In fact, in such instances lying is the right thing to do – we ought to lie.

Lying and breaking promises are highly likely to cause upset in many/most cases, as, in general:

- people do not like being lied to
- people want to be trusted and lying undermines this and weakens people's general faith in humanity
- lying frequently causes hurt when discovered
- lying often causes stress to the liar.

For these reasons lying comes with an inbuilt negative outcome, so the benefits of any 'good' lie need to outweigh these. Because of this it is generally wrong to lie and break promises.

So, although an act utilitarian would deny that truth-telling (and promise making) comes with an inherent moral obligation, they would acknowledge that truth-telling, in general, should be the default position.

Rule utilitarianism

The rule, *tell the truth* is one that will generally maximise utility. So, for a strong rule utilitarian, it is always wrong to tell a lie (the moral value of the act depends on whether it is in accordance with the rule).

A weak rule utilitarian would, in general, tell the truth, but occasionally lie if it was clear that lying would maximise happiness. For many people, weak rule utilitarianism is the position that best describes their intuitions. Few would argue that telling the truth is always the right thing to do.

Preference utilitarianism

Preference utilitarians focus on whether a lie would satisfy more preferences. This is significant, as most people have a preference to be told the truth, which further justifies the default position of truth-telling. However, there are times ('Did my speech go well?') when the questioner may prefer to be lied to, in which case, lying is the right thing to do.

For an act utilitarian a lie that goes undiscovered (for example, having an affair) may cause no harm. However, for a preference utilitarian the lie would go against someone's preference to be told the truth, regardless of whether the person finds out they are being lied to or not. So the moral weight of the lie starts immediately.

Exam checklist

You should be able to:	✓
Describe what is meant by utility and maximising utility	
Outline Bentham's utility calculus	
Outline and evaluate Mill's distinction between higher and lower pleasure (qualitative hedonistic utilitarianism)	
Outline and evaluate Mill's 'proof' of utilitarianism	
Outline and evaluate preference utilitarianism (non-hedonistic utilitarianism)	
Outline and evaluate the difference between act and rule utilitarianism	
Outline and evaluate the claim that pleasure is the only good (Nozick's experience machine)	
Outline and evaluate whether utilitarianism is consistent with fairness and individual liberty/rights (including the risk of the 'tyranny of the majority')	
Outline and evaluate problems with utilitarianism around calculating happiness/pain (including which beings to include)	
Outline and evaluate whether utilitarianism leads to issues around partiality	
Outline and evaluate whether utilitarianism ignores both the moral integrity and the intentions of the individual	
Apply utilitarianism to the issue of stealing	
Apply utilitarianism to the issue of eating animals	
Apply utilitarianism to the issue of simulated killing	
Apply utilitarianism to the issue of telling lies	

Kantian deontological ethics

A 'good will'

For Kant, a **good will** represents the only 'pure' good in the world and it is the source of all moral value.

Most of us pursue ends that we think of as 'good'; these could be happiness, intelligence or money. Kant argues that each of these supposed 'goods' can sometimes be bad. For example, someone may gain happiness from torture, or use intelligence to swindle money from pensioners.

For Kant, no 'end' that we pursue can be thought of as morally good in itself. Happiness, intelligence, money and so on can only be considered good if they are accompanied by, or result from, a good will. In this way, a good will is the source of good.

Also, *a good will is one which acts for the sake of duty*. In other words, in willing the action you are not motivated by a particular end or goal, but by the duty to do the right thing, which is to act in accordance with the moral law.

And it is the motive, not the consequence, that is key in assigning moral worth. Because of this, Kant's ethics are often labelled as being **deontological**. This is the general term for ethics that are based on duty.

Criticism: is a good will always good?

Is a good will always good? Well-meaning Billy tries to help everyone. But he is very clumsy and keeps accidently hurting people and breaking things as he helps others cross the road or carries their bags. After a while, people might question whether Billy's undeniably good will is such a good thing after all.

Acting in accordance with duty versus acting out of duty

Sometimes you can do the right thing (act in accordance with duty). But if you have the wrong motive then the act has no moral worth.

Kant gives the example of a shopkeeper who does not rip customers off because he wants a good reputation. For Kant, his actions are not moral. Not ripping off customers is the right thing to do, so he is acting in accordance with moral duty. However, the shopkeeper is not doing it out of a sense of duty for the moral law, but for his reputation. As such, his act has no moral worth.

In contrast, consider a poor shopkeeper who is struggling to make ends meet. This shopkeeper understands that being honest is the right thing to do and does not rip off customers for this reason. In this case his act is carried out out of duty, so has moral worth.

Sometimes you can be motivated both by the sense of duty and another goal (for example, enjoyment), where duty and interest coincide. This can make the motive of duty less clear to see, but as long as you are motivated by duty, then the act is a good act.

Revision activity

A five-mark question might ask you to explain Kant's distinction between acting in accordance with duty and acting out of duty. Practise explaining this with a suitable example.

Hypothetical versus categorical imperatives

When considering what to do there are different **imperatives** or suggestions that our reason puts forward as possible ways we ought to act. An imperative can be experienced as an inner 'tug' on our will – a reason that we should act in one way rather than another. There are two different types of imperative.

Hypothetical imperatives

This type of *ought/should* depends upon your having a certain goal, for example *If you want a cup of tea you should boil the water.* The first part of the **statement** gives us the condition we aspire to; the second part tells us what we should do to meet this condition. In other words, the *ought* is conditional upon the desire – which not everyone will have (not everyone wants a cup of tea).

Hypothetical imperatives are often linked to the word *good*, as in: *It is good to get your pawns out early in chess*, or *It is good to boil the kettle when making tea* – although *good* is not used in a moral sense here. This is because hypothetical imperatives are not moral imperatives, for example *It is good to wear gloves when you burgle a house.*

Kant is not really interested in hypothetical imperatives, as they are not moral imperatives. First, they lack the universality to be moral imperatives because they are based on desires/ends that not everyone shares. Not everyone wants a cup of tea, so it is not the case that everyone should boil a kettle.

Second, actions based on hypothetical imperatives are performed because we are trying to achieve some personal goal. As we saw in the previous section, actions motivated by personal goals have no moral worth. Only those motivated by a good will – a duty to do the right thing – count as moral actions.

Categorical imperatives

For Kant the moral law (like scientific laws) should be universal and apply to everyone – regardless of their particular desires. The sorts of imperative Kant thinks are central to morality are ones that are unconditional and absolute, or (in Kant's terminology) categorical.

An example might be, *You ought to keep your promises.* Note that this use is not dependent on any goals or aims we may have – the 'if you want X' bit of the imperative disappears, leaving only 'you ought to do Y'. These sorts of imperatives tell us that we have a certain obligation or duty regardless of the consequences. This is what is meant by saying they are unconditional or categorical. It is this sort of *ought* that Kant regards as the only genuinely moral *ought*.

Imperatives and reason

Kant believed that as rational beings, if we genuinely have the desire, and the imperative is a sound one, then we are rationally committed to follow it. For example, consider the hypothetical imperative: *If you want to lose weight, then you should exercise more and eat less.* Kant believed that if you genuinely do want to lose weight, then your reason commits you to exercise more and eat less. (Kant is sometimes accused of overlooking weakness of the will – when you accept the imperative and want the end, but still do not do it.)

Likewise, with **categorical imperatives** reason reveals that there are certain ways we should act and as rational beings we have a duty to act on these imperatives.

> **Revision activity**
>
> A three-mark (or five-mark) question might ask you to explain what a hypothetical or a categorical imperative is. Practise writing short, accurate answers with a suitable example.

Now test yourself answers at **www.hoddereducation.co.uk/myrevisionnotesdownloads**

The categorical imperative (first formulation)

Moral imperatives are categorical ones. For Kant there is one categorical imperative (although he gives several versions of it). Unlike hypothetical imperatives, categorical imperatives are not based on desires and 'ends', as they are not universal. Stripped of desires and 'ends', the categorical imperative can only be based on the idea of reason and rationality itself. It is the imperative that I should only act on principles that I can consistently universalise that other rational beings should follow.

> Act only according to that maxim [rule] whereby you can at the same time will that it should become a universal law without contradiction.
>
> Immanuel Kant, *Grounding for the Metaphysics of Morals* (1785) trans. J.W. Ellington, Hackett, 3rd edn (1993) p.30.

This is the categorical imperative (the universal law formulation). It is an imperative, as a rational being, to be logically consistent. Kant thinks that this imperative can be used as a test – a test we can use to work out how to behave morally. He gives several examples.

False promises – a perfect duty (to avoid)

A man needs some money. He intends to get hold of it by promising to pay it back, but with no intention of repaying. Can this be willed as a universal law without contradiction?

Step 1: Work out the underlying rule being followed (the **maxim**). Try to make the maxim as general as possible; something like: *When in need, make promises with no intention of keeping them to gain help.*

Step 2: Can you conceive of a world with this maxim as a law? What would happen if everyone followed this maxim and made promises they did not keep? Presumably no one would trust promises anymore. Kant argues that this maxim cannot be a universal law without contradiction. The man, in willing this maxim, is willing that we all live in a world with no promises, but simultaneously willing that he gains money via giving a false promise.

Because the contradiction happens at the conceiving stage, it is a contradiction in will and the maxim generates a perfect duty – in this case, a perfect duty *not* to do it. A perfect duty is one that we are always obliged to follow. We have a perfect duty to keep promises. Breaking a perfect duty is always wrong and your action would always be blameworthy.

Helping others – an imperfect duty

Someone is doing pretty well in life. He sees that others need help but is inclined not to help.

Step 1: The underlying maxim is something like: *I will not help those in distress, when I easily could, through selfishness.*

Step 2a: Can you conceive of a world with this maxim as a law? Kant thinks it is possible to conceive of a world where people don't help each other, so the maxim is not ruled out at this stage.

Step 2b: Can you rationally will that this be a universal moral law? Kant says 'no'. Everyone has been in situations (as a baby, for example) when they were unable to help themselves and needed the help of others, and we would not want to be in a situation where we need assistance and yet no one will help us. Because this maxim was conceivable as a universal law, but could not be consistently willed, it is a *contradiction in will*, which generates an imperfect duty – an imperfect duty not to not help others, which means that in situations when we can easily help, we cannot always ignore those in need.

Breaking an imperfect duty is not always wrong, and not always blameworthy. Quite how much of a duty this becomes – how much we should help others – is not very clear.

Revision activity

Can you explain the difference between a perfect duty and an imperfect duty?

The categorical imperative (humanity formulation)

REVISED

Kant argued that the ability to create and follow your own rules is what gives humans both reason and **autonomy** (which animals lack). Above we explored the universal law version of the categorical imperative, however Kant argued that this imperative can be conceived in different ways. A second version, the humanity formulation, takes this idea of autonomy as its central premise, requiring that we only ever*:*

> Act in such a way that you treat humanity, whether in your own person or in the person of any other, never merely as a means to an end, but always at the same time as an end.

> Immanuel Kant, *Grounding for the Metaphysics of Morals* (1785) trans. J.W. Ellington, Hackett, 3rd edn (1993) p.41

Kant believed that this has the same meaning as the *universal law* formulation, but presents the theory in a more intuitive way. It expresses the idea that it is always wrong to treat a person in a way that involves them in an action that they do not, in principle, have a chance to consent to.

This does not mean you can never use people as a means.
● Every time I take a taxi or call a plumber, I use a person to further my ends. However, this person has consented to the arrangement, and they too are using me as a means to an end – to make money.
● The moral problem arises when you do not have a chance to consent, so your autonomy/rationality is undermined. When this happens, you are being used *merely* as a means to an end.

For example:
● A woman buys your old bass guitar. She deliberately gives you fake £20 notes.
● This action is wrong because the woman is bypassing your autonomy.
● If she told you the notes were fake, you would not accept them. In keeping it secret, she is acting in a way that does not give you a chance to consent.
● She is treating you merely as a means to get the guitar and not as a person with your own ends.

So, stealing from me, lying, deceiving, drugging, kidnapping, forcing me into slavery or murdering me (and so on) would be to involve me in acts that I have not had the opportunity to consent to. In doing any of these, the person would be using me merely as a means to further their own ends, and not as an autonomous being with my own ends.

Imperfect duties

Earlier (page 69) we saw that we have an imperfect duty to help others (according to the universal law formulation). Refusing to help others does not breach the humanity formulation directly (it does not override anyone's autonomy), but it is not in harmony with the formulation. Being in harmony requires us to help develop autonomy/rationality in ourselves and others, so we have an imperfect duty to do this (meaning we should help others sometimes).

Human dignity

The humanity formulation places a great emphasis on respecting autonomy, which for many people is the key to dignity. The modern conception of human rights shares this feature too and Kant's ethics were influential in their formation.

Consider this example. When in a relationship, Amy and David took some nude pictures of each other. After splitting up, David posted some of the pictures of Amy on social media as revenge. This is wrong. Why? Utilitarians may struggle to explain why (because the photos may bring happiness to others), but could argue that this goes against a rule that itself maximises happiness.

For Kant, though, this represents a violation of the supreme moral principle: human autonomy. Amy is being treated as a means to an end and not as a person with ends herself. She has had no opportunity to consent. David has a perfect duty not to act in the way he did. Kant's theory seems to cut right to the core of what is wrong in this situation.

Revision activity

Consider the case of the theft of £20 from a random jacket hanging on the back of a chair. Use the categorical imperative – both the universal law and the humanity versions – to argue why this is wrong.

Issues with Kantian deontological ethics

Clashing/competing duties

For Kant, we are all creators of our own moral laws. The categorical imperative enables us to work out what is morally permissible and what our moral duties are. Using this system, we can create our own metaphorical book of moral laws. However, just because a maxim gets into our book, that alone does not tell us where it goes and what weight to attach to it.

What happens when our duties seem to contradict each other?

Consider the case of the axeman asking where your friend is. Kant, most agree, would say that it is wrong to lie. You cannot universalise lying. However, we also have a duty to care for others, so we might see this axeman scenario as a clash in our duties. A perfect duty to tell the truth, and an imperfect duty to care for others. In general, perfect duties have no exceptions, and imperfect duties do not have to be performed all the time. So this gives us some direction.

For Kant, however, clashing rules represent a serious problem. His whole moral system involves not acting on rules that cannot be consistently universalised. Inconsistent rules give rise to duties (a duty **not** to follow the rule), so duties are all about consistency. If it is the case that two moral duties are rationally inconsistent, then, by definition, they cannot be duties.

So, for Kant, duties cannot clash, by definition. However, we can sometimes be wrong in thinking through our grounds of obligation. If I made a promise to a friend that I would lie for them, then it would seem that I have two conflicting duties: (A) I should keep my promises, and (B) I should never lie. However, it is clear that I am not obliged to keep the promise in this case; we cannot rationally will a maxim whereby we keep promises to lie. It was wrong to make this promise; in fact, we have a duty not to make such promises. In this case, revisiting my grounds of obligation shows that the duties do not in fact clash, as I do not have a moral duty to keep this promise.

Competing imperfect duties

The situation is less clear when imperfect duties are included, such as our imperfect duties to help others, to develop our own talents and so on. These are duties we do not have to follow all of the time. This seems to leave us with a very vague moral duty. Having an imperfect duty alone does not seem to tell us when to perform the imperfect duties. Also, knowing which of these duties to prioritise can be difficult, and sometimes these duties seem to compete.

Utilitarians seem to have an advantage here, as by using the common currency of happiness, they can weigh up different actions and see how they compare. Kant's approach is less clear; instead of looking at the consequences, we need to examine our reasons – our grounds of obligation – and see which are stronger.

This approach is not easy to follow, and Kant does not offer much guidance, but it can be argued that this complexity is just part of the world that we live in. After all, human rights lawyers spend years arguing about the hierarchy of competing rights. Does freedom of speech mean I can say anything? What about when it undermines other people's right to practise religion? Or if I incite hatred, might this undermine people's right to freedom of movement? And so on.

Now test yourself answers at **www.hoddereducation.co.uk/myrevisionnotesdownloads**

Not all non-universalisable maxims are immoral (and not all universalisable maxims are moral)

Another criticism is that the link between **universalisable**/non-universalisable maxims and morality is not very clear.

Not all universalisable maxims are moral

Many trivial acts, which do not seem to be moral, can be successfully universalised. For example: *I will chew food 32 times before eating, to aid digestion.* However, for Kant, those maxims that *can* be universalised are just morally permissible; we have no duty to do them. It is those actions that we *cannot* universalise that generate moral duties (a duty not to perform them). This, though, leads to the criticism that Kant's ethics only tell us what we *cannot* do (lie, deceive and so on); it does not give a positive account of what we *should* be aiming for. On the other hand, this can also be seen as a strength in that it allows for people to pursue their own projects and ends.

Are all non-universalisable maxims immoral?

Something odd happens when we try to universalise maxims that include relative or 'norm'-related positions (comparing ourselves to others). For example, consider the maxim, *When taking an exam, I will try to come in the top half.* This seems reasonable, yet a world where this is a law is impossible to conceive, as we cannot all, by definition, be in the top half. This would mean we have a perfect duty not to try to come in the top half (nor the bottom 50 per cent too!).

I can, however, universalise the maxim, *When taking an exam, I will always try to gain over half of the marks, to push myself,* as everyone could get over half the marks. The problem lies in fixing outcomes in relation to other people in ways that cannot be universalised. Perhaps we should never compare ourselves to others. Maybe this is to treat them as a means to an end. Nevertheless, on the face of it, acting on the maxim of coming in the top 50 per cent does not seem to be immoral.

Similarly, consider this rule: *I will always help the poor when I can afford to, to ease their plight.* It can be argued that this cannot be willed to be a universal law, as if everyone did this, there would be no poor. So we have a duty to *not* help the poor! However, this would seem wrong. Here we seem to have a clear case where a non-universalisable maxim is not immoral to act on. Indeed, we *should* help the poor, even though it seems we cannot universalise the maxim.

Trivial duties

The categorical imperative seems to generate trivial duties. Consider the rule, *On Halloween, I will go and collect sweets, but will not provide any at my house, to save money.* I can conceive of a world where this is the rule (it would be a dull Halloween!), but I cannot rationally will it, as following the maxim would destroy the institution of 'trick or treat', on which the maxim relies. But, although I cannot universalise just collecting sweets, this does not seem to be a moral issue – just an issue of cultural practice. (Many of Kant's examples of perfect duties involve acting in a way that would undermine a social/cultural institution that the act also relies on – for example, promising. In the case above, the institution is 'trick or treat', which does not seem to be a moral one.)

Do we have a duty to offer sweets at Halloween if we also collect them? According to Kant, it might seem so. But if this is not a moral duty, then how can we distinguish moral duties from non-moral duties, unless we have a prior understanding of what morality is – an understanding that is not derived from the ability to universalise maxims?

The moral value of consequences REVISED

One of the key objections to Kantian ethics is that it places all of the moral worth on the motives of an action – just as utilitarianism is criticised for placing all of the moral worth on the consequences! It seems our moral intuitions want to have it both ways – to attach some of the value to the consequence and some to the motive.

Consider the case of the murderous-looking axeman asking the whereabouts of your friend.
● For Kant, it would be wrong to lie, as you cannot consistently conceive of a world in which this is the moral law.
● The apparent requirement to lie seems very counter-intuitive. There may be various Kantian ways of avoiding this seemingly counter-intuitive conclusion, but the fundamental point seems to be that telling the truth will have bad consequences – and this is what makes it wrong, not whether you can universalise the maxim underlying the act.
● On this occasion, the moral value of the act (lying or not) seems to reside in the consequence, not the motive.

Kant's larger claim, in essence, is that we all need to focus on our own sphere of control: make sure that *I* do not lie, deceive and so on, and only act on maxims that *I* have worked out to be universal laws. If we all did this, then we would end up in a world where we all had freedom and autonomy.

However, in the example above, I might be busy doing the right thing, but the mad axeman certainly is not, and this would have disastrous consequences. This focus on being consistent seems to miss the bigger, and consequentialist, picture. It can appear that Kantian ethics are more concerned with being rationally consistent in our actions, than with whether a friend is killed.

Consequentialist?

On a different note, Kantian ethics is also criticised for having consequentialist tendencies (while claiming to be purely motive-based). Some suggest that to work out whether a maxim can be consistently willed relies on thinking through the consequences of having this as a law – and so is consequentialist. However, in Kant's defence, the moral value lies in the consistency of the will, and not in whether the world would be 'good' or 'bad' if the maxim were universalised.

The value of certain motives such as love, friendship, kindness REVISED

Take this example:
● Parent A enjoys reading to their daughter and spending time with her.
● Parent B does not enjoy these things but does so out of duty to do the right thing.

- A common intuition is that Parent A, who helps their daughter because they want to, is the better parent.
- Kant, however, argues that only Parent B's actions have moral worth, as they are carried out from duty, not desire.
- This seems counter-intuitive. We seem to want to place value on the motive of Parent A too, and more generally also on the motives of people who *want* to help others and devote their life to doing so.

For Kant, these actions, though in accordance with duty, are not done for the sake of duty, so have no moral value. This seems to be at odds with our intuition that certain emotions have a moral dimension, such as love, compassion, guilt and sympathy, or pride and jealousy. Do we not regard the possession of such emotions itself as morally praise- or blameworthy, as having moral value?

Friendship

Imagine you were ill in hospital for a few weeks and a good friend kept visiting. You ask the friend if they find the visits boring – she reveals that she doesn't like visiting, but only does so out of a sense of duty. How would you feel? Would you think that the friend's visits had greater moral worth than those of a friend who enjoyed coming to visit you, or valued your friendship?

Some object to Kant's approach, claiming it encourages a cold and calculative approach to ethics by demanding that we put aside our feelings for the suffering of others. In Kant's defence, he is not against people *wanting* to do right actions, and positive emotions, but he is clear that acting only from desire, not duty, has no moral worth.

We cannot adopt an impersonal perspective

Some doubt whether it is possible for us to set aside the interests, concerns and desires that make us individuals, and to think of ourselves, as Kant wants us to, as purely rational autonomous beings engaged in universal law-making.

Bernard Williams argues that the impartial position that Kant wishes us to adopt may be possible for factual considerations, but not for practical, moral deliberations. For example, if I ask, 'I wonder whether strontium is a metal?' it is possible to remove the personal 'I' from this question, and seek an answer that is independent of my own perspective on the world.

This kind of deliberation means that it is possible for anyone to take up my question and be given the same answer; there is what Williams calls a 'unity of interest' in the answer. This is because deliberation about facts is not essentially personal, but is an attempt to reach an impersonal position (where we all agree that these are the facts).

In contrast, Williams maintains that practical deliberation is essentially personal, and it does make a difference whether it is me or someone else (for example, the madman's mother, his intended victim, the victim's life insurer or the madman himself) asking the question, 'Should I lie to this man?' We cannot and should not strive for the same impersonal position as in the factual case. With moral deliberations there is no longer a 'unity of interest', and a different person, with a different set of desires and interests, who is now standing in my shoes, might seek a different answer.

Morality is a system of hypothetical, not categorical, imperatives (Foot)

REVISED

Philippa Foot argues that moral systems cannot ignore desires, for example the desire to help others. Without such motives, we do not have a good reason to behave morally.

She argues that the moral law, as Kant conceives it, does not give sufficient reason to follow it. Only end-based, 'hypothetical' imperatives give sufficient reasons to act.

Consider these hypothetical imperatives:
● If you want to win the match, you ought to practise.
● If you want to earn loads of money, you should work in the City.

In these cases (and for all hypothetical imperatives), the reason to act is clearly given – because you will win the match/earn lots of money. Your action is motivated by an end/goal.

Categorical imperatives cannot motivate

However, for categorical imperatives, the reason to act on them is not evident. Kant argues that using reason we can work out the right thing to do independently of whether you have any particular desire/end (for example, *you ought to help others*). But, stripped of desire, what is the reason to obey the 'ought'?

Foot rejects different possible 'reasons' to act on categorical imperatives:
● *To be rationally consistent.* Foot suggests that 'The fact is that the man who rejects morality because he sees no reason to obey its rules can be convicted of villainy but not of inconsistency.' ('Morality as a system of hypothetical imperatives', p. 310).
● *We are 'bound by moral law'.* However, we are not literally bound/ pulled. Even metaphorically, these terms do not really apply to morals, as I cannot escape the binding/pulling when it comes to ropes, but can when it comes to morality. Foot suggests the metaphors of 'binding' are illusory – an attempt to give the moral 'ought' a magical force.
● *Out of respect for the moral law.* But we do not have to behave morally out of respect for the moral law, any more than we have to follow etiquette for the sake of convention.

In rejecting the idea that moral oughts somehow magically 'command' us all to act, Foot pre-empts Mackie's argument from queerness (**page 102**).

Morality as hypothetical imperatives

Foot argues that we should reject the theory of psychological hedonism, which claims that we always act out of self-interest.
● Some people genuinely want to help others, not for their own benefit, but just to help others.
● Likewise, some genuinely care about justice, liberty and fairness.
● If we accept that these are suitable moral goals, then we have the proper motivation to be moral. Indeed, some people fight hard for liberty and justice; these can be highly motivating ends.

So, moral oughts are not categorical but hypothetical oughts, depending on 'if' you have the relevant moral ends.

Is moral obligation universal?

The downside to this is that moral oughts are not universal, but contingent on you believing the specific moral ends are worth pursuing. Surely morality applies to all of us and you cannot escape the duty of morality by claiming to not have moral ends/desires?

In defence, Foot argues that no one can really 'escape' morality, as we are all raised in a society that encourages moral behaviour and punishes immorality.

But does having morality as a universal duty help us? Foot suggests that the idea of universal/categorical 'oughts' casts humanity as forced conscripts in a moral army. A better vision is to see us not as conscripts, but as 'volunteers banded together to fight for liberty and justice and against inhumanity and oppression'.

Foot sees morality as a series of hypothetical imperatives: *you should not steal*, *you should help others* and so on. You might have some of these moral ends, but not others. There is no single overall imperative to be moral. Collectively, this series of imperatives constitutes morality.

> **Revision activity**
>
> Philippa Foot's paper is quite long and complex. Practise summarising her key points and find a way of memorising the content.

Applied Kantian ethics

Stealing

REVISED

Stealing is morally and legally wrong for Kant for the following reasons.

CI (categorical imperative) universal law formulation

What would happen in a world where people acted on the maxim, '*Steal when in need*'? The concept of property and ownership would break down, so stealing, as such, would not exist. In acting on the maxim you would be simultaneously willing that there is a world in which property (and so stealing) exists and also a world in which property (and stealing) does not exist. It is therefore inconceivable to act on this maxim and you have a perfect duty not to steal.

CI – humanity formulation

By stealing (and not asking to have) you are bypassing the owner's autonomy, so treating them as a means to an end. You have a perfect duty not to steal.

Kant's political theory

Imagine a world without laws – Kant calls this 'a state of nature'. It would be unsafe – we would lack freedoms and have no rational means of settling disputes other than by violence.

In a civil society (Kant calls this 'a rightful condition'), we have laws which enable us to co-exist and we can settle disputes with reason, not violence. As rational beings we have a duty to seek to live in a rightful condition. If you choose to break the law and steal, you move us all towards a state of nature. This cannot be consistently willed.

> **Exam tip**
>
> When discussing Kant's ethics, remember to be clear about when you are applying the universal law formulation of the categorical imperative or the humanity formulation. It might seem pedantic, but it is a part of showing knowledge and being accurate in your explanations.

Eating animals

REVISED

Kant argues that reason enables humans to transcend their animal instincts. Through reason we can work out what we ought to do – both what is prudent, given our desires, and what we morally ought to do. Following our own rules (both prudential and moral) gives us autonomy.

Animals lack autonomy. They are driven by instinct and cannot work out, through reason, what they *should* do. Animals act on the world, but they do not 'will'. Because they cannot conceptualise what they should do, animals do not pursue ends and therefore we do not have to treat them as beings with ends themselves – as beings with moral status. The moral law only applies to those beings capable of making moral laws.

However, Kant does not think this gives us licence to be cruel to animals.

> If a man shoots his dog because the animal is no longer capable of service, he does not fail in his duty to the dog, for the dog cannot judge, but his act is inhuman and damages in himself that humanity which it is his duty to show towards mankind.
>
> Kant, *Lectures on Ethics,* trans. and ed. P. Heath and J. Scheewind, Cambridge: CUP (1997) p.240

Kant believed we have a duty to perfect our own moral nature and this involves an imperfect duty to sympathise with the suffering of other creatures and to 'cultivate the compassionate natural (aesthetic) feelings in us'.

This may rule out some particularly cruel farming methods – but only for the farmer, as it is *his* duty to work towards moral self-perfection that is potentially threatened. It would not be morally wrong for the consumer to eat the meat.

Criticisms

Kant's argument relies on the premise that being cruel to animals makes a person treat others with less moral respect. This is debatable. Some research shows that those who are violent towards animals are more likely to be violent towards humans. However, establishing a link does not show that being cruel to animals *causes* people to be cruel to humans. There could be an underlying condition that causes the cruelty both to animals and humans.

Being cruel to animals is only wrong because of a duty to ourselves, not the animal. This seems counter-intuitive. Surely the animal's suffering is morally relevant.

People with several mental impairments may also being unable 'to will' – to rationally pursue ends. Does this mean that such people lack moral status too?

Now test yourself

The quote about shooting a dog is relevant to the sections on treatment of animals and on simulated killing (below). Make sure that you can explain it clearly. What perfect and imperfect duties do we have that are relevant to the point of the quote?

TESTED

Simulated killing

REVISED

Universal law formulation

Can I universalise the maxim '*Engage with simulated killing when I want to be entertained*'?

On the surface, it seems both conceivable and consistent to will this to be a universal law. This would make such entertainment morally permissible.

However, the arguments relating to cruelty to animals (above) may also apply here. What if being entertained by simulated killing makes us less compassionate towards others? Kant argued that we have an imperfect duty to cultivate compassionate feelings in ourselves. After all, we cannot consistently will things that make us less compassionate as we have all benefited from the compassion of others. Maybe we have a duty not to entertain ourselves in this way.

The argument hinges on whether there is a causal connection between simulated death as entertainment and being less compassionate to humans. The evidence does not have to directly suggest that such activities make us more violent, just that it makes us less compassionate (though violence would be an indicator of this).

The evidence is mixed. Also, remember that demonstrating a link does not necessary show a causal link. Although society has become less violent in the last twenty years, studies have shown that general empathy levels have decreased during this time. The cause of this is not clear, and commentators are keener to suggest that wider societal changes in capitalism and parenting are bigger factors than films/video games.

Humanity formulation

When I watch a violent film, or play a violent game, on the face of it I do not seem to be overriding anyone's autonomy. The actors chose to be in the film. The pixels on the video screen are not real people. Some may be offended by such sights, but if such films are not shown in outdoor places, where they cannot be avoided, then people's autonomy (their choice to not watch) is not being overridden.

However, using the argument (above) it can be argued that to be entertained by simulated killing is not in harmony with the humanity formulation as it may make us inclined to treat others with less compassion.

Telling lies

REVISED

Can you universalise a maxim of telling lies?
- The whole concept of lying relies on the concept of truth-telling.
- If everyone lied, then lies would not deceive.
- In using the maxim '*Lie to gain advantage*', the liar would be willing a world in which there are no lies (as everything is deception), but also relying on the existence of lies.
- This is inconceivable, so you have a perfect duty not to lie.
- Lying also undermines the autonomy of the listener. You are not treating them as a person with ends.

The case of the deranged axeman asking about the whereabouts of a friend is discussed a lot in relation to Kant, in part because he wrote about a similar example. Kant claimed you have a duty to tell the truth. Most find this conclusion very counter-intuitive.

Can a Kantian lie?

First, note that there is no moral requirement for you to speak at all. You could simply stay quiet and so avoid lying. However, in Kant's version he stipulated that you are forced to answer by the axeman.

But surely we can universalise a maxim such as *I will lie if it saves an innocent person's life*. In real life people do lie, but truth-telling still exists, so willing that sometimes lies occur is not inconceivable. Kant says that maxims should be as general as possible, but narrowing lying to circumstances such as this seems legitimate and morally relevant.

Also, the maxim could be consistently willed as I would be happy to be lied to/about in these circumstances. Further, we have an imperfect duty to help others, so not only is lying morally permissible, it may also be the right thing to do.

On the humanity formulation the axeman is clearly aiming to undermine the autonomy of someone else. He has chosen to leave the rightful condition and enter a state of nature (**page 77**) and seems intent on settling matters by force not reason. In doing this he has given up his entitlement to be treated as a person with full autonomy and so we can lie to him. (In a similar vein if someone attacked you, Kant would say that defending yourself is permissible.)

Explaining Kant's insistence on truth-telling

So why did Kant say to tell the truth to the axeman? One interpretation argues that Kant wrote about not lying to the axeman in a paper discussing the law. If you lie to others, then you are either breaking the law directly (for example, insurance claims) or could be held legally responsible if events turn out badly (for example, telling someone that a bridge is safe when it isn't). However telling the truth is always legally right. Maybe Kant was only making a legal point in his paper.

> **Revision activity**
>
> Kant's position on telling the truth to the axeman seems counter-intuitive. Can you articulate why he might have said that? What contrasting 'Kantian' positions can be taken to justify lying to the axeman?

Exam checklist

You should be able to:	✓
Describe what is meant by a good will	
Explain the difference between *acting in accordance with duty* and *acting out of duty*	
Explain the difference between *hypothetical imperatives* and *categorical imperatives*	
Outline and apply the universal law formulation of the categorical imperative	
Explain the difference between *perfect* and *imperfect duties*	
Outline and apply the humanity formulation of the categorical imperative	
Outline and evaluate the claim that some duties can clash/compete	
Outline and evaluate the claim that not all non-universalisable maxims are immoral (and not all universalisable maxims are moral)	
Evaluate Kant's theory in light of the counter-claims that the consequences determine moral value	
Outline and evaluate the claim that Kant's theory does not take into account the value of certain motives such as love, friendship, kindness	
Outline and evaluate Philippa Foot's criticism of Kant that morality is a system of hypothetical, not categorical, imperatives	
Apply Kantian ethics to the issue of stealing	
Apply Kantian ethics to the issue of eating animals	
Apply Kantian ethics to the issue of simulated killing	
Apply Kantian ethics to the issue of telling lies	

Aristotelian virtue ethics

Introduction

Virtue ethics focuses on the person, and their character, rather than on individual actions. It is 'agent-centred' rather than 'act-centred' (see **page 52**), asking 'what sort of person should I be?' Within virtue ethics the most important thing is that we develop positive character traits (called virtues) such as generosity, courage and honesty. Aristotle (384–322BC) developed his theory of virtue ethics in his book *Nicomachean Ethics* (or *Ethics*).

Revision activity

Read the section above **(pages 51–52)**. Draw a diagram that shows the main differences between virtue ethics, Kantian ethics and utilitarian ethics.

Aristotle's account of the 'good'

'The good' for human beings

REVISED

Aristotle holds a **teleological** view of the universe, believing that everything in the universe is directed to some final goal, or 'good'. Aristotle starts the *Ethics* by arguing that there is an ultimate good for human beings:

P1 Everything we do is aimed at some good.
P2 Each good is also done for the sake of a higher good.
P3 This cannot go on forever (otherwise our aim would be pointless).
C Therefore there must be an ultimate good, which everything we do is aimed towards.

The purpose of the *Ethics* is to identify the ultimate good for us as humans (which Aristotle outlines in Book 1) and how we can achieve it (which Aristotle details in Books 2 to 10).

Criticisms

1 Some actions appear to have no purpose or good (day-dreaming, doodling), which undermines P1.
2 The argument may commit the fallacy of composition similar to 'all human beings have a mother, therefore there is one mother that all human beings have' (see *My Revision Notes, AQA A-level Philosophy Paper 2*, Section 1 Metaphysics of God).

Exam tip

When you explain a concept it helps to give a relevant example; Aristotle gives the example of bridle-making. List some examples of your own which illustrate Aristotle's argument above.

The meaning of *eudaimonia* as the 'final end'

REVISED

Two approaches lead Aristotle to the conclusion that **eudaimonia** is the ultimate good/final end.

1 An empirical approach: assessing popular opinion tells him that the ultimate good/final end is *eudaimonia* ('flourishing' or 'happiness'). But Aristotle rejects popular ideas about what *eudaimonia* is:
  ○ Pleasure? (no, as this would make us just animals)
  ○ Wealth? (no, as this is just a means to an end)
  ○ Honour? (no, as this depends on other people's recognition)
  ○ Goodness? (no, as this is compatible with a life of suffering)
  ○ Contemplation? (Aristotle returns to this later, see **page 87** below)
2 A conceptual approach: analysing the concept of 'ultimate good/final end', Aristotle concludes it must be:
  a an end, never a means to an end
  b the 'most final' of final ends, for the sake of which everything else is done

Revision activity

Go through each of the candidates above (pleasure, wealth, honour, goodness, contemplation) and for each one assess which criteria they meet and which criteria they fail.

c self-sufficient, so nothing could be added to it to make it even better

d the most desirable of all things.

Aristotle concludes that *Eudaimonia* meets all of these criteria and so is the final end.

Eudaimonia is the good life, or 'living well and faring well'. The table below explains further what *eudaimonia* does/doesn't mean.

What *eudaimonia* IS NOT:		What *eudaimonia* IS:	
A means to an end	✗	The final end, the supreme good, for the sake of which everything else is done	✓
Something we are born with, or which we suddenly 'get'	✗	Something we work hard to achieve – through actions that develop our character	✓
Completely within our control	✗	Partly out of our control – affected by both good and bad luck (e.g. being born in a time of civil war, or born in peacetime)	✓
Mere 'happiness' (a short-term, subjective, pleasure-based experience)	✗	'Flourishing' (a process or an activity that continues throughout our life)	✓

The relationship between *eudaimonia* and pleasure

REVISED

According to Aristotle, hedonist philosophers such as Eudoxus are wrong and the good for humans is not pleasure:

- Pleasure does not meet the criteria above (the final end etc.).
- We are more than just pleasure-seeking animals.
- There are other things we aim for (virtue) that do not necessarily bring us pleasure.

However, the good life does involve pleasure, and philosophers who reject pleasure as an important part of *eudaimonia* are also wrong. So Aristotle's theory falls midway between two extreme views:

- Hedonism: pleasure IS the good.
  - Aristotle's *Ethics*: pleasure is a PART of the good.
    - Asceticism: pleasure plays NO part in the good.

So Aristotle argues that pleasure is a good, but it's not '*the* good'. Aristotle is clear that we should avoid excessive indulgence in physical pleasures. But enjoying physical pleasures is something Aristotle sees as a virtue – and its opposite (shunning all physical pleasure) is a **vice**.

For Aristotle, pleasure also plays a crucial role in developing virtues of character, and so enabling us to reach *eudaimonia*. Initially we may not enjoy being generous, courageous, honest etc. But as we start to act as a virtuous person (and not just go through the motions) we start to enjoy and get pleasure from being generous etc. In a significant way pleasure completes the activity.

In his final conclusion of the *Ethics*, Aristotle argues that the most pleasure we can gain is from theoretical reasoning (contemplation) and philosophy.

The function argument: virtues and function

The 'function argument' is used by Aristotle to show that *eudaimonia* is only achieved through exercising our reason. The first part of Aristotle's argument aims to show that humans have a particular function (or 'characteristic activity').

P1 Every type of person has a distinctive role/function in society; and every part of the body has a distinctive function.

P2 Therefore human beings must also have a distinctive function.

P3 Our function cannot be growth/nutrition (shared with plants) or sentience (shared with animals) – as these are not distinctive to humans. Being guided by reason is distinctive to humans.

C1 Therefore our function is to live guided by reason.

Criticisms of the first part

1 Aristotle seems to use a weak **argument from analogy** to show that humans have a function: 'just like parts of the body, and just like roles in a society, humans must have a function'.

2 Aristotle may also be guilty of the fallacy of composition again: 'every part of a human has a function; therefore the whole human must also have a function'.

The second part of Aristotle's argument aims to show that in order to function well (and reach *eudaimonia*) we need to develop the right qualities/virtues.

P4 X is good if it fulfils its function well.

P5 X fulfils its function well if it has the right qualities (virtues).

P6 Therefore a good human is someone with the right qualities (virtues) which enable them to live guided well by reason.

P7 The good life of a human (i.e. *eudaimonia*) = the life of a good human (i.e. someone with virtues enabling them to be guided well by reason).

C2 Therefore *eudaimonia* is reached by someone with the right virtues which enable them to be guided well by reason.

So if we use reason well then we will live well, and to do this we need to develop all the necessary virtues. Our virtues are determined by that which defines us as human (our 'blueprint') which Aristotle calls our soul. Aristotle concludes that *eudaimonia* as an activity of the soul in accordance with virtue.

Aristotle analyses, and divides up, the soul as follows:

Non-rational part of the soul		Rational part of the soul	
Growth and nutrition	Desire and emotion	Practical reason	Theoretical reason
	Influenced by reason		

Through exercising our reason, and using reason as our guide, we can develop virtues within each part of the soul. Virtues are usually thought of as character traits relating to our emotions or our desires – resulting in **dispositions** such as courage, honesty, generosity etc. But there are intellectual virtues of practical reasoning (practical wisdom, **page 87**) and of theoretical reasoning (contemplation).

Revision activity

Draw the soul using Aristotle's divisions and sub-divisions.

Aristotle's account of virtues and vices

Virtues as character traits or dispositions

REVISED

Humans have habitual ways of behaving/reacting/feeling, and these dispositions form our character. When reason guides our emotions and desires, then over time we develop positive dispositions or character traits – called virtues (*arete*) – which enable us to reach *eudaimonia*. When reason fails to shape our emotions/desires we develop flawed character traits – called vices.

> **Revision activity**
>
> Write a list of virtues and vices. Memorise it so that you can draw on it for examples in your exam.

The role of education and habituation in the development of a moral character

REVISED

Virtue is not innate. Humans have the potential to develop virtues, but we have to develop these character traits over time: through learning them as children, and as adults through commitment, practice and habit (or 'habituation'). But a virtue is more than a habit (which can be 'absent-minded') since virtue requires reasoning when we act.

The skill analogy

REVISED

Aristotle compares developing a virtue with developing a skill. We are not born with a skill, but have the capacity to learn that skill: we can only learn the harp by first playing a harp; we can only learn to become brave by first performing brave acts.

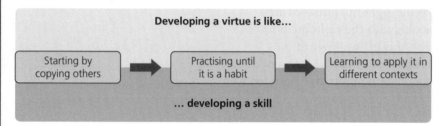

Figure 2.2 **The skill analogy**

To be virtuous you must: a) act in a virtuous way and b) act as a virtuous person acts, i.e. you choose to act for the right reasons, and are consistent over time in your choice, even in new or complex situations. This is closely connected with practical reasoning (**page 87**).

The importance of feelings

REVISED

Aristotle gives a central place to feelings in his moral theory. All our actions are a display of some emotion: desire, anger, fear, confidence, envy, joy, hatred, longing, pity, etc.

1 Virtue means expressing the right/appropriate amount of these feelings, neither too much nor too little but 'in the mean'.
2 A virtuous person has no inner conflict; they don't have to overcome their feelings in order to do the right thing.

The doctrine of the mean and its application to particular virtues

Virtue lies between displaying 'too much' and 'too little' of a particular feeling – this is the doctrine of the mean. For example fear and confidence are natural responses to dangerous situations. Displaying too much fear is cowardly; displaying too much confidence is rash. Reason helps us be driven by the right amount of fear/confidence – and we then act courageously. If we continue to do this over time then we develop the virtue of courage. People with very many virtues, and no vices, have what Aristotle calls 'excellence of character' or 'moral virtue' (*ethica arete*).

A genuinely courageous person uses reason to assess a situation and knows exactly when to be brave, when to run away, and when to be bold. So the 'mean' is about doing the right thing, at the right time, to the right people in the right way – Aristotle calls this the 'mark of virtue'.

> **Exam tip**
>
> The 'mean' is not a prescription telling us to 'act moderately'. Aristotle talks about the mean as being relative to the individual – the right (mean) amount of food for an elite athlete is different from the right amount of food for everyone else.

Criticism

Aristotle's doctrine of the mean packages our emotions too neatly. Each feeling is supposed to be exhibited in a character trait that can be 'too much', 'too little' and 'the mean'. But these quantities aren't always on a single scale, for example cowardice (fear), rashness (confidence) and courage; and Aristotle says some things have no mean (for example, murder).

Aristotle's account of moral responsibility

Voluntary actions

For Aristotle, moral responsibility is tied to whether an action is freely chosen or not. Understanding which acts are freely chosen will help us make moral judgements (and assign praise/blame), and also help us understand which actions are relevant to virtue/character development.

A voluntary action is an intended action. Only voluntary actions contribute to our character and virtues (see **page 86**). A voluntary action is one that we:
- intend to do and the origin of the action lies within us
- carry out in full knowledge of what we are doing
- freely choose.

If a knowing, intended action flows from our desires, then this is still freely chosen: it is wrong to say we have been 'forced' to act by our desires. We must bear full responsibility for our voluntary actions.

Involuntary actions

An involuntary action is one that is contrary to our intention. Aristotle identifies two types of involuntary actions: those done in ignorance (which he calls non-voluntary actions – see below) and those done under compulsion. Actions done under compulsion fall into two categories: straightforward types and more complex 'mixed' types.

	Acts done under COMPULSION	
	Straightforward cases	**'Mixed' (more complex) cases**
Examples	1. A sailor is blown off-course by the wind. 2. A sailor is taken off-course by being kidnapped.	3. A sailor is told to commit a robbery otherwise their children will be murdered. 4. A sailor dumps their cargo overboard during a storm to avoid sinking.
Is there intention?	**No.** In these simple cases of compulsion the sailor goes off-course, but the origins of this are entirely external and the sailor contributes nothing.	**Yes and no.** Aristotle calls these 'mixed' because **a)** at the exact moment of action the sailor was in control and intended to act in this way; but **b)** the sailor felt compelled and did not *really* choose or intend these actions.
Is the sailor responsible?	**No.** There is a lack of **agency**, and because of this Aristotle argues we should not be held responsible (neither praised nor blamed).	**Yes.** There is some agency, some choice, and so we are responsible and can be praised or blamed. But judgements should take into account the circumstances – and so we could be forgiven and pardoned.

Non-voluntary actions

REVISED

A non-voluntary action is unintended because it is done from ignorance. For example, the Greek tragic hero Oedipus did not know that he killed his father and then married his own mother. There are many ways in which we are ignorant when we act – we don't know all the facts, we misinterpret or misunderstand the situation etc.

Are we responsible for non-voluntary actions? This depends on how we behave after we find out the facts:

- If there is regret and we wish we had acted differently, then the action was contrary to our intention (involuntary). We would still be responsible but we could be forgiven and pardoned.
- If there is no regret and we would not have acted differently, then we should be judged and held fully responsible as if this were a voluntary action.

> **Revision activity**
>
> Draw a chart or diagram showing the connection between voluntary, involuntary and non-voluntary action according to Aristotle.

Aristotle's account of the role of practical reason and action, and of pleasure

The relationship between virtues, actions and reasons

REVISED

Our virtues are dispositions built up from voluntary actions. But not all voluntary actions are relevant to judging character (for example, acts done on the spur of the moment or by young children). Voluntary actions relevant to virtue are the result of a special kind of internal reasoning process – choice. An action is chosen if it is the result of prior deliberation. What we deliberate about has to be within our control (for example, Spartans cannot deliberate about the types of government that Scythia should have).

There is a feedback loop between reasons, actions and virtue that can be illustrated as shown in Figure 2.3.

> **Revision activity**
>
> List and memorise all the ways in which reason is relevant to *eudaimonia* in Aristotle's virtue ethics.

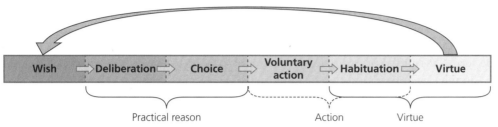

Figure 2.3 The feedback loop

The role of practical reasoning/wisdom

REVISED

Aristotelian and other types of virtue ethics give us no simple rules on how to behave. Instead virtue ethics requires us to have a number of practical reasoning skills that mean we will make the right decision in each situation we encounter. These skills include:

- the ability to deliberate
- understanding the situation we're in
- judging what we need to do, deciding on a choice
- the cleverness to accomplish our choice.

In order to reach *eudaimonia* we need to practise and do these things well – developing the intellectual virtue called practical wisdom. But practical wisdom is not possible without excellence of character (honesty, generosity, courage etc.) as these virtues of character establish the right goals/ends/wishes while the virtue of practical wisdom gives us the best chance of achieving those goals (see also Figure 2.3 above).

Criticism

Aristotle changes direction in Book 10 concluding that *eudaimonia* is best achieved through contemplation/philosophy. This conclusion is problematic as contemplation is a narrow kind of life, whereas developing practical wisdom and virtues of character imply a diverse, exciting, challenging and varied life – much more like a good life than just doing philosophy!

> **Revision activity**
>
> Draw a diagram showing the connection between 'practical wisdom', virtue and the good life.

Issues with Aristotelian virtue ethics

Does virtue ethics give clear guidance about how to act?

REVISED

Mill's principle of utility and Kant's categorical imperative provide rules about how to act, but Aristotle's ethics has no such clear rules. The doctrine of the mean does not tell us to 'act moderately in every situation'; it tells us to 'do the right/virtuous thing in every situation'. This is unhelpful as we want to know exactly what the right thing to do is. Aristotle himself admits that knowing what we need to do is very difficult, writing that it is not easy 'to feel or act towards the right person to the right extent at the right time for the right reason in the right way'.

However, virtue ethics accepts that every situation is different and moral rules always have exceptions. In response to the complexity of moral situations virtue ethics requires us to be thoughtful and act virtuously and to practise and repeat this. So there is some guidance, namely to develop:

1 virtues of character (for example, courage)
2 practical wisdom.

> **Exam tip**
>
> When explaining these five issues you could spend one or two introductory sentences (but no more) putting them into the context of Aristotle's overall theory, to help show why they are problematic.

Rosalind Hursthouse argues that virtue ethics gives further guidance on how to act. We know which virtues we should strive to develop and which vices we should avoid. For Hursthouse, these can be turned into rules for action, which she terms 'v-rules'. For example, the virtue of honesty entails the v-rule 'do what is honest' and the vice of cruelty entails the v-rule 'do not be cruel'.

Criticism

Different cultures may value different character traits, suggesting that virtues and vices are relative – and **relativism** raises further issues for Aristotelian virtue ethics (see **page 101**). However, James Rachels argues that there are some universal virtues (honesty, loyalty, generosity, courage) valued by all societies – which would entail universal v-rules.

Can virtue ethics deal with clashing virtues?

REVISED

Moral theories can be tested against 'hard cases', that is, moral dilemmas. For Aristotle's theory these occur where virtues conflict with each other. For example, someone you love who has a painful terminal illness may plead with you to help them die. The virtue of charity motivates you to help them towards euthanasia, the virtue of justice forbids you from killing them.

> **Revision activity**
>
> Write down two further examples of situations in which there are clearly clashing virtues.

Virtue ethicists have a number of ways of resolving the clash. They can:

1 explain how the conflict is only apparent and that practical wisdom will help determine which virtue is the *right* (most appropriate) virtue to exhibit in this situation
2 propose a hierarchy of virtues; Aristotle, for example, would put justice above charity
3 admit (as Rosalind Hursthouse does) that sometimes there is no resolution of the clash, but at least virtue ethics recognises the impact this has on us. Helping someone in pain to die or allowing them to live is a decision that leaves us with a residue of pain, guilt or regret. Hursthouse calls these emotions the 'moral remainder' and only virtue ethics is sophisticated enough to recognise this as morally significant.

The possibility of circularity

REVISED

Aristotle tells us that a virtuous act is one done by someone who is virtuous. But how can we identify who is virtuous? According to Aristotle, virtuous people are those who do virtuous actions. So the definition contains the term being defined! The circularity can be clearly seen here:

A virtuous act (X)	= an act done by a virtuous person (Y)
A virtuous person (Y)	= someone who habitually performs virtuous acts (X)
Therefore a virtuous act	= 'an act done by someone who habitually performs virtuous acts'

This circular definition is problematic because it does nothing to help explain the nature of virtuous actions/people. However, Aristotle does introduce other elements into his explanation of both concepts which could resolve this issue.

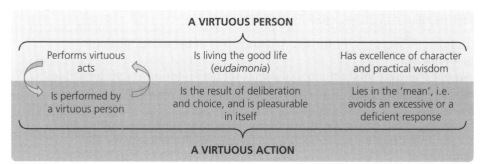

Figure 2.4 Avoiding circularity

These additional elements mean that circularity can be avoided: for example, a virtuous person habitually performs actions that are the result of deliberation and choice and which bring pleasure, and which avoid exhibiting 'too much' or 'too little' feeling.

Must a trait contribute to *eudaimonia* in order to be a virtue?

REVISED

In his function argument Aristotle is clear that we cannot live the good life for humans (*eudaimonia*) without being a good human (and having virtues). So by being virtuous I contribute to my own *eudaimonia*. But is it possible to have a virtue that doesn't contribute to *eudaimonia*?

Aristotle thinks not – for him all virtues contribute to *eudaimonia*, whether they are virtues of character or the intellectual virtues.

But there have been other accounts of virtue ethics over the past 2500 years. For example, David Hume (1711–76) gave a non-Aristotelian account of those positive character traits which we call virtues. Hume makes no mention of *eudaimonia*, but argues that we approve of virtues because of either their utility or their agreeability. For Hume these virtues arise from our sympathy for other people. So on Hume's account a trait does not need to contribute to *eudaimonia* in order to be a virtue.

The individual and the moral good

REVISED

Moral philosophy, as we are familiar with it, draws a distinction between actions that are self-interested (good for the individual) and actions that benefit others (morally good). But is Aristotle's virtue ethics primarily a self-interested theory, a moral theory, or can it be both (see the table below and overleaf)?

Aristotle's ethics is about the good for the individual...	Aristotle's ethics is about the moral good...
<ul><li>The *Ethics* is very clearly an account of how we can each flourish and live a good life.</li><li>Some of Aristotle's virtues benefit only the individuals possessing them: traits like being ambitious, proud and aristocratic.</li><li>Even intellectual virtues like practical wisdom are also self-interested in that they help me to reach *eudaimonia* for *myself*.</li></ul>	<ul><li>Aristotle believes he has shown that what is truly good for the individual is to strive for a life of virtue.</li><li>Many virtues we would immediately recognise as 'moral' (in the modern sense), such as justice, generosity, truthfulness, friendliness, courage etc. as they benefit those around us.</li><li>Aristotle is very clear that some behaviours (which we all recognise in modern terms as 'immoral'), such as murder and theft, are never appropriate in any circumstances. ⇨</li></ul>

In Aristotle's ethics the good for the individual = the moral good

- Within the ancient Greek tradition of Socrates, Plato and Aristotle, moral behaviour does not conflict with self-interested behaviour.
- We must be careful to follow our *true* self-interest, not our apparent self-interest. Aristotle argues that we are wrong if we think that what is good for us is a life of pleasure, or wealth or honour – these do not lead to *eudaimonia*.
- The good life is a thoughtful, considered, active life, in which we develop virtues which generally will benefit both ourselves and other people – so as each of us flourishes individually we all flourish collectively as a community.
- This individual pursuit of proper self-interest towards virtue and *eudaimonia* thus results in what modern philosophers would call 'the moral good'.

Applied ethics: Aristotle

Introduction

Both Kantian and utilitarian approaches to ethics are able to provide principles or rules which guide our actions and tell us what we ought to do. Aristotle's virtue ethics does not provide such clear rules (see **page 87** above), but some virtue ethicists like Rosalind Hursthouse think that simple rules can be generated (v-rules) which tell us to 'act courageously', 'act honestly', 'don't act cruelly' etc.

Applying virtue ethics to moral problems is harder and more nuanced than applying Kantian or utilitarian approaches – but this makes Aristotelian virtue ethics more like the real-life experience of a moral dilemma, and its complexity is its strength. Aristotelian virtue ethics requires us to draw on virtues of character (for example, generosity, courage, honesty) as well as the intellectual virtues of practical wisdom (for example, deliberating skills, understanding situations, strong judgement). When making a moral decision or judgement about a dilemma a virtue ethicist should:

- consider the context/circumstances (are there any special rules or roles that apply here?)
- consider the range of choices available to the agent
- consider the virtues that are drawn on in this situation (both intellectual and moral virtues)
- consider the vices that must especially be avoided in this situation
- consider the long-term effect on someone's character
- analyse, weigh up, and make a final decision – the action should be the right one at the right time, made in the right way and the right manner towards the right person.

> **Exam tip**
>
> Be clear in the exam when you are drawing on Aristotle's original work (under 'what does Aristotle say?') and when you are drawing on the ideas of contemporary Aristotelian virtue ethics (thinkers like Hursthouse and Annas).

Stealing

REVISED

What does Aristotle say?

Consider the mean – from a strict Aristotelian perspective there is no right time or manner (etc.) for stealing. Theft is never in a mean, and it is always unjust because it deprives other people of what is their fair share. But a contemporary virtue ethicist using an Aristotelian approach might address the issue of theft with more flexibility.

What would a virtue ethicist say?

Consider the context of the action. In the *Rhetoric* Aristotle acknowledges that magistrates need to take circumstances into account when examining the actions of a thief. Take the example of Robin Hood who robs from the rich and gives to the poor, but within the context of an unfair society.

Consider both moral *and* intellectual virtues. If Robin Hood possessed the virtue of practical wisdom, then he would have assessed the options he had in order to achieve his goal, and chosen the right one (in his case stealing from the rich). If Robin also possessed a virtuous character then his act of theft must have sprung from the right goal – the virtues of benevolence or charity – and he would have performed the theft *because* of his benevolence/charity (not because he wanted to impress Maid Marian, or embarrass King John).

Consider what other choices are available. The Aristotelian virtue ethicist would ask whether other virtuous actions were available (for example, setting up a charitable trust instead of robbing the sheriff, or running an apprenticeship scheme for the wayward youths of Sherwood) that might achieve the same goal while avoiding the vice of theft. The virtue of practical wisdom is needed to weigh up these options.

Consider the long-term effect on someone's character. If this theft is a one-off action then it won't become a habit/trait; but if this is part of a pattern of criminal behaviour then the virtue ethicist may urge Robin to find an alternative outlet for his charitable urges.

Simulated killing

REVISED

Simulated killing is an imitation of killing and may be 1) something we watch as an audience, or 2) something we take part in as a player.

What does Aristotle say?

Is it wrong to watch a killer? Enjoying watching characters die on screen or on stage seems morally problematic even though they are fictional. However, in his *Poetics* Aristotle wrote about how watching a tragedy (often ending in death) is cathartic for the audience. Emotions in the audience build up throughout the play (or film) until there is a climactic scene triggering a cathartic release and the emotion is gone. This safe 'cleansing' of negative emotions is seen by Aristotle as part of the education of our character. By watching tragedy and killings on stage/screen we can practise feeling the right emotion, at the right time etc. and so help the development of virtue.

What would a virtue ethicist say?

Is it wrong to play a killer? Matt McCormick argues that playing and enjoying violent video games is morally problematic. As computer games have become more realistic, the possibilities for simulated killing have become more graphic, more numerous and for many people, more upsetting. McCormick argues that a Kantian and a utilitarian approach are inadequate for accounting for what may be wrong with simulated killing – as they only focus on the (minor) real-world impact of playing such games.

Consider the long-term effect on someone's character. For McCormick only virtue ethics can articulate what is morally objectionable about murdering people with a car in a video game which has few real-world consequences. Employing Aristotelian ethics, McCormick concludes that 'engaging in simulated immoral acts erodes one's character, and makes it more difficult for one to live a fulfilled *eudaimonic* life'. Building a virtuous character requires careful cultivation, and the habitual cruel or callous behaviour of killing in video games moves people away from virtue, not towards it.

Eating animals

What does Aristotle say?

Aristotle's response to the question of 'whether animals should be eaten or not' is straightforward and is based on his view of the moral status of animals. Although Aristotle recognised a continuum between humans and other animals – like animals we grow, eat and perceive – unlike animals we have the capacity for reason and virtue. So in his hierarchy of living things he places humans above other animals and argued that: 'Plants exist for the sake of animals, and the other animals for the good of humans … for our service and our food.'

What would a virtue ethicist say?

Consider, and weigh up, all relevant virtues and vices. Rosalind Hursthouse argues that the practices of modern factory farming (for example, debeaking chicks, breaking their legs, force-feeding geese etc.) are undeniably cruel. Moreover, we do not actually need factory-farmed meat to survive, so the deaths of over 15 billion chickens a year are a result of human desire and pleasure (and possibly greed) rather than of necessity. Our failure to exhibit compassion is a vice, tolerating a system of cruel farming practices is a vice, and our failure to be less greedy (less intemperate) is a vice. So for Hursthouse eating factory-farmed animals is the opposite of virtue.

> **Revision activity**
>
> What virtues, and what vices, are exhibited in eating organically farmed animals? What might a virtue ethicist conclude on the basis of this?

Telling lies

What does Aristotle say?

In his analysis of the virtue of truthfulness, Aristotle describes it as a mean between someone who boasts or exaggerates too much, and someone who is too self-deprecating. Here Aristotle is thinking of 'truthful' as honesty about yourself. But when we are discussing the morality of lying we are usually interested in dishonesty (or honesty) when talking about the world and Aristotle condemns such falsehoods as 'bad and reprehensible'.

> **Key quote**
>
> Falsehood is in itself bad and reprehensible, while the truth is a fine and praiseworthy thing.
> Aristotle, *Ethics*, Book IV, section 7

What would a virtue ethicist say?

Consider honesty. All forms of virtue ethics require us to develop an honest character. We flourish as individuals if we are honest, and we flourish together as a community if we are honest and can be trusted in the information we exchange, the promises we make, the judgements we cast. Honesty, and dishonesty, are both habits and a virtue ethicist emphasises how every single day we can build our moral character by practising honesty and by avoiding dishonesty and telling lies.

Consider habits and actions. Aristotle sees virtue as habits emerging from actions that are 'voluntary', i.e. intended. Voluntary actions are made from choice and deliberation (when done well this is practical wisdom), while avoiding acting in ignorance. If our understanding of the situation is based on lies, then this makes it difficult for an action to be genuinely voluntary, and so harder for us to develop habits and virtue.

Consider the context of the action. There may be an occasion when doing the right thing (finding the mean) entails telling a lie. Practical wisdom will enable us to determine when the general rule 'be honest, don't lie' can be bent or broken. Peter Geach gives the example of St Athanasius who was able to find an alternative to lying (not telling the truth but without actually lying), and so we should look at our range of possible options and only lie in the last resort. The Kantian example of your neighbour, the axe murderer, asking for his axe back – the one you borrowed – is straightforwardly, and common-sensibly, solved by virtue ethics. Here is a situation where the right and virtuous thing to do is to lie – so long as this doesn't develop into a habit.

Exam checklist

You should be able to:	✓
Explain what 'the good' is for human beings according to Aristotle	
Explain the meaning of *eudaimonia* as the final end	
Outline and explain the relationship between *eudaimonia* and pleasure in Aristotle's ethics	
Evaluate Aristotle's function argument	
Outline and explain the relationship between virtues and function in Aristotle's ethics	
Explain and illustrate virtue as a character trait or disposition	
Explain the role of education/habituation in the development of moral character	
Evaluate the skill analogy	
Explain the importance of feelings in Aristotle's virtue ethics	
Evaluate the doctrine of the mean and explain how it applies to particular virtues	
Outline and explain the difference between voluntary, involuntary and non-voluntary actions	
Outline and explain the relationship between virtues, actions and reasons	
Explain the role of practical reasoning in Aristotle's virtue ethics	
Explain the difficulties for Aristotelian virtue ethics:	
● that it does not give sufficiently clear guidance about how to act	
● how it resolves clashing or competing virtues	
● how circularity arises from Aristotle's definition of a virtuous act and a virtuous person	
● whether a trait must contribute to *eudaimonia* to be a virtue	
● what the relationship is between the good for the individual and moral good.	
Explain how Aristotle's virtue ethics can be applied to the following issues:	
● stealing	
● simulated killing	
● eating animals	
● telling lies	

Meta-ethics

Introduction

Meta-ethics is an investigation into what morality is. This includes examining:

- the meaning of moral concepts and ethical judgements, like good/bad/right/wrong/virtue/vice
- what the origins of these concepts are
- whether they refer to anything in the world (such as moral properties or moral facts).

The origins of moral principles: reason or emotion/attitudes or society?

REVISED

What are the origins of morality?		
Reason	Emotions/attitudes	Society
For example, social contract theories	For example, moral sense theories	For example, moral relativism
For example, Thomas Hobbes (1588–1679)	For example, David Hume (1711–76)	For example, Karl Marx (1818–83)
In a 'state of nature', we all suffer as everyone pursues selfish interests, many through violent means. In order to escape this, the rational thing to do is for us to cooperate. We agree to give up some power and freedom by submitting to social rules enforced by government. So moral rules (don't kill, help others etc.) may originate as a rational choice: if we are each less selfish then we each will benefit.	Hume argued that morality comes from our feelings of sympathy towards others. Hume believed we get pleasure from actions which bring about pleasure in someone else, or diminish their pain. So from these feelings of sympathy (and the pleasures that this brings us) we develop virtues, habitual actions that help others and ourselves.	Relativists (see **page 101**) observe that each society develops its own moral codes. Marx also took a relativist view, arguing that moral systems are an 'ideology', a set of normative beliefs constructed by those in power. In the case of morality, these rules may vary over time and place, but in each society those rules ensure that the powerful maintain their position of power.

The distinction between cognitivism and non-cognitivism about ethical language

REVISED

Cognitivists and non-cognitivists disagree about whether ethical language (for example, sentences like 'killing is wrong') can be true/false. Cognitivists argue that sentences like these express beliefs and so are **propositions** which are 'truth apt', i.e. have a truth value (either true or false). Non-cognitivists argue that moral sentences are not propositions, neither true nor false, but instead they have another function – for example, acting as prescriptive commands.

Now test yourself answers at **www.hoddereducation.co.uk/myrevisionnotesdownloads**

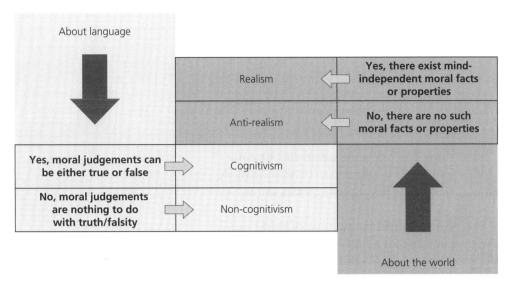

Figure 2.5 Cognitivism and non-cognitivism, realism and anti-realism

Realists and anti-realists disagree about whether there is anything 'out there' in the world to which our moral concepts, like good, actually refer. Realists argue that there are 'real' moral properties or 'real' moral facts which exist independently of human minds. Anti-realists argue that no such properties exist and that moral terms refer to something else, for example the expression of an emotion.

Exam tip

You need to be clear about the overlap between realism/anti-realism and cognitivism/non-cognitivism for each theory of language you study. See the table below.

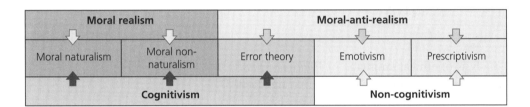

Moral realism

Moral naturalism (cognitivist)

REVISED

Naturalism is a type of **moral realism**, arguing that moral properties/facts are natural properties of the world (not supernatural or divine properties). Moral **naturalism** leads to a cognitivist view of moral language, since our ethical judgements are true or false insofar as they correctly (or incorrectly) refer to those natural properties of the world.

Utilitarianism

A common form of moral naturalism is utilitarianism. Jeremy Bentham (1748–1832) argued that all humans aim to secure pleasure and to avoid pain – these are psychological, and hence natural, properties. Following from this descriptive fact he draws a prescriptive conclusion, namely that 'we ought to maximise pleasure and minimise pain'.

John Stuart Mill (1806–73) also begins his 'proof' of utilitarianism with a natural fact, namely that happiness is what each person desires. He then appears to conclude that happiness is 'the good' because each person's happiness is desirable, i.e. it ought to be desired. G.E. Moore criticises

Mill for arguing 'desired = desirable = good', and for appearing to reduce moral terms like 'good' to natural terms, like 'desired' (see **page 97**). Moore may have misunderstood Mill here.

Virtue ethics

Aristotle's virtue ethics may be based on natural facts but it is not a theory that reduces moral terms to naturalistic properties. However, Aristotle's theory is naturalistic to this extent:

- For Aristotle 'the good' is the thing humans most value, and we can empirically determine this by looking at what people strive for, namely to live the best possible life: *eudaimonia*. This is a natural fact about human behaviour.
- For Aristotle, 'the good' can be determined by the type of thing we are. He argues that to live the good life for a human you need to live as a good human. To be a good human means fulfilling your function well. Our function is a natural fact about us – it is our distinctive activity – which for humans is to be guided by reason. So using our reason (which is a natural fact) is bound up with the moral good.

Moral non-naturalism (cognitivist)

REVISED

Moral non-naturalism is the claim that there are moral properties/facts in the world but that these aren't natural properties – they are special, non-natural properties. So non-naturalism is a form of moral realism, and it leads to a cognitivist view of moral language, as our ethical judgements refer (truly or falsely) to these non-natural properties.

Intuitionism

G.E. Moore's (1873–1958) analysis of ethical language in *Principia Ethica* led him to conclude that naturalism, and utilitarianism, are wrong about moral judgements. Moore argued that, in contrast to utilitarianism, we cannot sense moral properties nor can we argue for them on the basis of evidence. Moore maintains 'the **autonomy of ethics**' – in other words that ethical judgements are unique and cannot be analysed in non-moral or natural terms.

If moral properties are not natural, then how do we come to discover them? Moore argues that moral truths, such as 'killing is wrong', are grasped as self-evident intuitions – and his theory is known as **intuitionism**.

Moore believes he can show naturalism to be deeply flawed through both his open question argument and his identification of the **naturalistic fallacy**.

Moore's open question argument

For Moore, terms are either definable (such as 'bachelor') or indefinable. We can double-check a definition with further questioning (see table below). If our double-check leads to a closed question (i.e. one you can answer only with either a 'yes' or 'no') then we have found a genuine definition. If our double-check leads to an open question (requiring further investigation) then we have not found a genuine definition.

Definition	Double-checking the definition	Open or closed question
1 A bachelor is an unmarried man	Is an unmarried man really a bachelor?	Closed
2 Good is maximising utility	Is maximising utility really good?	Open

So for Moore, if we genuinely can define 'good' as X, then asking 'But is X really good?' would be a closed question (as in example 1 above). Yet 'Is X really good?' is actually an open question which means that 'good' is indefinable, and that meta-ethical theories like naturalism (which reduce moral terms to natural properties) are wrong.

The naturalistic fallacy

The naturalistic fallacy identified by Moore as a further problem for moral naturalism, is just a special form of a more general fallacy, namely:
- A term that is indefinable cannot be defined.
- Any attempt to define the indefinable is fallacious.

When Moore applies this to naturalism it becomes the naturalistic fallacy.
- Good is indefinable (it is simple and unanalysable).
- Utilitarians (and other moral naturalists) attempt to define the good in natural terms.
- Hence utilitarianism is guilty of the naturalistic fallacy.

Criticism

Moore may have misunderstood Mill's argument. Mary Warnock (1924–) argues that Mill does not define 'good' or 'desirable' – he simply informs us that people already consider happiness to be good (and desirable). It is an empirical observation and it does not entail that Mill thinks good = happiness.

Moral naturalism	
Strengths of the theory	**Possible criticisms of the theory**
Removes need for reference to anything supernatural or divine	Overly reductive – reducing complex moral terms to simple natural properties
Enables us to determine what is right and wrong	Guilty of the naturalistic fallacy?
Accounts for how moral disagreement is possible	Guilty of Moore's open question argument?
Accounts for our intuition that morality is universal and objective	Guilty of moving from an 'is' to an 'ought'? (page 100 below)
Leads to a clear (cognitivist) account of how ethical language is meaningful	Doesn't account for some of our experience of morality as subjective or relative

Moral non-naturalism	
Strengths of the theory	**Possible criticisms of the theory**
Enables us to determine what is right and wrong	Moral facts exist in a mysterious moral realm
Accounts for our intuition that morality is universal and objective	Mill may not be guilty of the naturalistic fallacy
Leads to a clear (cognitivist) account of how ethical language is meaningful	We don't experience moral truths as 'self-evident'
Preserves the 'autonomy of ethics'	Some experience morality as subjective or relative
Avoids reducing moral terms to natural terms	Is wrong in its analysis of the meaning of moral terms (see Emotivism, page 103)

Issues with moral realism

Hume's fork

REVISED

David Hume was an empiricist and a sceptic who took a careful and analytical approach to philosophy which made him doubtful of grand, metaphysical claims about God, reality and ethics.

Hume makes an important distinction between two ways in which we can properly reason and find out truths about the world. This distinction has become known as 'Hume's fork'.

	Hume's fork	
	1. Relations of ideas	2. Matters of fact
Subject matter	Mathematics, geometry, logic	Science, observations and generalisations about the world
Examples	'3 + 4 = 7' 'All bachelors are unmarried men'	'Barack Obama was a US President' 'Water can turn into ice'
How do we know?	Known *a priori* … by thinking about concepts alone	Known *a posteriori* … by experience
Ways in which sentences are true	True by definition, or tautologies (Kant calls these 'analytic truths')	True because of the way the world is (Kant calls these 'synthetic truths')
Degree of certainty	Certain (to deny them is a contradiction)	Not certain (it is conceivable to deny them)

How does Hume's fork present a problem for moral realism? Moral realists are cognitivists and believe moral judgements can be true or false. Hume's fork tells us the only two possible ways in which a moral judgement could be true or false.

In what way are moral judgements true or false?		
Are they relations of ideas?	No	Moral judgements are not tautologies. They are not certain (they can be denied without contradiction).
Are they matters of facts?	No	Moral judgements are not matters of fact – we cannot 'see' that killing is wrong.
Conclusion	Moral judgements are neither true nor false.	

So if Hume is correct, and moral judgements are neither true nor false, then moral realism collapses. Hume instead sees moral judgements as referring to our feelings of approval or disapproval when we see virtuous or vicious actions.

Ayer's verification principle

REVISED

A.J. Ayer (1910–89) was a logical positivist, part of a group who were inspired by David Hume. The logical positivists adopted a scientific approach to philosophy, aiming to define what is meaningful and put an end to the metaphysical nonsense of some philosophers. Ayer developed a principle similar to Hume's fork but, where Hume was concerned with knowledge, Ayer focused on meaning. Ayer's **verification principle** (VP) distinguished meaningful statements from nonsense as follows.

A sentence is meaningful if and only if:
- it is a tautology (that is true by definition) *or*
- it is verifiable through sense experience.

What Ayer's principle is asserting is that in order to say something is meaningful we must know what makes our statement true (how to verify it). Ayer believed that if a statement is not a tautology, and if there is no empirical way of discovering its truth, then it is meaningless.

For Ayer all moral judgements fail the principle: for example, 'stealing is wrong' is not true by definition, and it cannot be verified by any empirical investigation (we cannot 'see' or 'intuit' wrongness). So Ayer goes further than Hume because Ayer argues that moral judgements have no meaning at all:

P1 Only statements that meet the verification principle have meaning.

P2 Moral judgements do not meet this principle.

C Therefore moral judgements are meaningless.

Ayer is a non-cognitivist about moral language and his theory of **emotivism** (**page 103**) views moral judgements as expressions of our feelings of approval/disapproval. If Ayer is correct then moral judgements are neither true nor false (thus **cognitivism** is wrong) and they do not refer to any mind-independent properties/facts (thus moral realism is wrong).

Criticism

It is commonly noted that the most straightforward version of Ayer's verification principle fails its own criteria – as it is neither true by definition nor empirically verifiable. By using a flawed conceptual tool (the VP), Ayer may be wrong in his analysis of moral judgements.

Hume – moral judgements are not beliefs

REVISED

Hume's empiricist approach to ethics led him to explore moral psychology, and to ask 'what is it that motivates us to act morally, or virtuously?' His account of moral motivation leads him to conclude that moral judgements (for example, 'helping people is good') cannot be beliefs and his argument can be summarised as follows.

P1 Moral judgements, such as 'it is good to help other people', motivate us to act. (The technical term for this is 'internalism', and this theory of motivation stretches back to Plato and Aristotle.)

P2 Beliefs and reason can never motivate us to act. (This is known as the Humean theory of motivation – see below.)

C Therefore, moral judgements cannot be beliefs.

The Humean theory of motivation is based on Hume's analysis of beliefs/reason and of human psychology. Imagine that moral judgements are founded on beliefs and reason – then we would be motivated by either relations of ideas or matters of fact (Hume's fork). But relations of ideas do not motivate us – simply understanding mathematical or logical relationships doesn't drive us to action. Nor do matters of fact motivate us – knowing what is true or false about the world is helpful but it doesn't make us take action by itself. There is something else in our psychological make-up that drives us to action.

Reason and belief are important as they give us a picture of what the world is like (what is true, and what is false). But knowing what's true

> **Exam tip**
>
> Using technical philosophical terms (like 'internalism' or 'the Humean theory of motivation') can add depth to your examination answers. But you should make sure that you really do understand the technical term – as using it incorrectly (for example, writing the 'Human theory of motivation') can have the opposite effect.

about the world (for example, that there is marmalade at the back of the fridge) doesn't lead to action. What is needed is desire (what Hume calls 'affections' and 'passions'), such as really wanting a marmalade sandwich. These passions lead to action (hunting down the marmalade).

Therefore, according to Hume it is our passions, not our reasons, that drive action. Hume concludes (C, above) that if moral judgements do drive actions (i.e. P1), and reasons and beliefs cannot drive actions (i.e. P2) then reasons and belief cannot be moral judgements.

If Hume is right then moral judgements cannot be true or false (as they are not beliefs), in which case cognitivist theories of ethical language are incorrect. Moreover, if Hume is right, then moral judgements have their source inside us, in our emotions, passions and desires – and so moral judgements do not represent something independent to us, they do not refer to external moral properties or facts. In which case moral realism is incorrect.

> **Key quote**
>
> Reason is, and ought only to be, the slave of the passions.
> Hume, *A Treatise of Human Nature* 2.2.3.4

Hume's is–ought gap

REVISED

In his *Treatise of Human Nature* Hume identifies what has become known as '**Hume's law**'. We can derive this law from the following argument:

P1 Judgements of reason describe what *is* the case.

P2 Judgements of value prescribe what *ought to be* the case

P3 Judgements of reason and judgements of value are therefore entirely different from one another – there is a gap between 'is' and 'ought'.

C Therefore you cannot draw conclusions about value ('ought') based on premises about reason ('is'), i.e. you cannot derive an 'ought' from an 'is' – this is known as Hume's law.

In the *Treatise* Hume observes that all the moral theories he's encountered break this law, for example utilitarians start by making observations about the world (that everyone desires their own happiness) and conclude with moral rules (that everyone's happiness ought to be desired). If Hume is correct then utilitarians cannot make the move from psychological hedonism (**descriptive**) to ethical hedonism (**prescriptive**).

Hume is making a simple logical point. No matter how much factual information I provide you with about some state of affairs, you cannot legitimately conclude (on factual grounds alone) anything about what ought to be the case. This is because the 'ought', as Hume says, 'expresses some new relation or affirmation'. So Hume's claim is a straightforward claim about what can and cannot legitimately be done when constructing an argument: a conclusion must be based solely on what is in the premises, it cannot suddenly smuggle in new information.

> **Now test yourself**
>
> Consider how you might utilise the meta-ethical concept of Hume's law in the following argument within applied ethics: 'Humans have always eaten animals, and have evolved to digest meat. Therefore humans should continue to eat animals.'
>
> TESTED

Hume's law (the **is–ought gap**) presents a problem for cognitivism on the following grounds:

P1 Cognitivists claim that moral judgements are true/false.

P2 If cognitivism is correct, then it would be possible to infer a moral judgement (which can be true/false) from descriptive statements (which can be true or false).

P3 But it is not possible to infer moral judgements from descriptive statements (which can be true/false). This is Hume's law.

C1 Therefore moral judgements are not true or false.

C2 Therefore cognitivism cannot be correct.

Criticism

John Searle (1932–) has argued that there are exceptions to the claim that you cannot derive an 'ought' from an 'is'. Consider:

P1 You promised to pay me back my £5 (an 'is').

C So you should pay up (an 'ought').

This argument seems perfectly in order. The fact that you have made a promise seems clearly to imply that you ought to keep it, and so suggests that it is possible to bridge the is–ought gap.

How might Hume react to an example like this in defence of his law? One thing he might try is to find some hidden evaluative premise. Is there a hidden premise here so obvious that it seems not worth stating? For example, here the hidden premise might be that 'we ought to keep our promises'; in which case the 'is–ought' gap remains.

Mackie's arguments from relativity and from queerness

REVISED

In *Inventing Right and Wrong*, J.L. Mackie aims to show that morality is not objective, it is subjective, and that moral realism is incorrect as there are no moral properties or facts that exist independently of us. Mackie's attack on moral realism is based on two arguments.

The argument from relativity

Mackie's argument from relativity can be presented as an abductive argument (to the best explanation):

P1 There are differences in moral codes from society to society (moral judgements appear to be made relative to each society).

P2 Accompanying these radical differences are disagreements between people about moral codes.

P3 Disagreements may occur between people either because:
- **a)** there is an objective truth about the matter, but people's perceptions of it are distorted

or

- **b)** there is no objective truth about the matter.

P4 Moral disagreements may occur between people either because:
- **a)** there are objective moral values, but people's perceptions of these are distorted

or

- **b)** there are no objective moral values, they are simply reflections of different ways of living.

C The best explanation of moral disagreements is that there are no objective moral values.

So for Mackie, the different moral codes between societies are best explained by viewing those codes as the products of a particular society in a particular context. If this relativistic view is correct then there are no objective moral values and moral realism is incorrect.

Criticism

Perhaps there are, in fact, common ethical principles present in all societies (don't kill, steal or lie, and look after your kin). This may be evidence that the moral realist is correct in saying that these fundamental principles are objective and not relative.

Now test yourself

How might you use Mackie's meta-ethical observations about relativism in a discussion within applied ethics about whether it is wrong to eat animals?

TESTED

The argument from queerness

Mackie's second argument is that if moral realism is correct then the world must contain two peculiar features:

1 Metaphysical queerness

Mackie is an internalist (see **page 99**) in believing that one of the essential features of moral values is that they provide motivation to action. Therefore according to Mackie, moral realism is committed to a belief (a) in the existence of strange objective moral properties in the world and (b) that these peculiar moral properties are somehow able to generate a motivation for action. Mackie argues that this absurd position is a good indication that moral realism is wrong. It is our needs, desires, hopes etc. that motivate us, not bits of the world 'out there'.

2 Epistemological queerness

According to Mackie, the moral realist must also be committed to believing that we have a mysterious faculty which enables us to detect these peculiar moral properties. G.E. Moore talks about 'intuition', and other moral realists must also require us to have this strange 'moral sense' which no one can point to or explain or even name. Mackie calls this 'lame,' because simply asserting that we have a special moral sense is inadequate as an explanation. Mackie's conclusion is that a far simpler explanation is that there are no objective moral properties – and so no need for any special faculty or sense.

Moral anti-realism

Mackie's error theory (cognitivist)

REVISED

Anti-realism takes the view that there are no moral facts or properties that exist independently of human minds. This type of meta-ethical theory often overlaps with **non-cognitivism** – the claim that moral judgements are *not* statements that refer truly or falsely to the world. Emotivism and **prescriptivism** are forms of anti-realism that are non-cognitivist. However, J.L. Mackie is an anti-realist about moral language (see **page 95**) who developed a cognitivist theory.

Mackie's ontological claim

In *Ethics: Inventing Right and Wrong*, Mackie argues for the bold claim that there are no objective moral values. Something is objective if:

It's either true or false, *or*

It's about the world 'out there', *or*

It describes something that is mind-independent

For Mackie, moral judgements cannot be objective in any of these ways because moral properties do not exist out in the world.

This part of Mackie's argument is known as his 'ontological claim' because it is an argument about what objects do or don't exist ('ontological' is the study of existence) out there in the world. His conclusion that there are no moral properties is based on his arguments from relativity and from queerness (see above).

Mackie's semantic claim

For Mackie *all* of our ethical judgements (not just those of moral philosophers!) include a claim to objectivity. This is an error.

● It is *not* a linguistic error, i.e. we are not misusing language, or misunderstanding how language can be used when we make moral judgements (which is what Ayer and Hare argue, see below).

● It is an error based on our belief in objective, independent, moral properties that literally do not exist.

● The error arises from the way we are brought up in society, which leads to a complex moral theory that we then *project* onto the world – as if it were true of the world. We 'objectify' the social arrangements that we've learnt ('you must do this' or 'don't do that') into moral codes. Note that this objectification is helpful for our societies, because it gives their rules of behaviour an authority which they would otherwise lack!

● This mistake persists because we believe that our projections of moral values onto the world are inherent in the world itself. So whenever we make a moral judgement we are making a claim about the world that is false.

This permanent error that we fall into when we make moral judgements gives Mackie's theory its name: **error theory**. Mackie's position is analogous to an atheist who argues that religious statements refer to the world, but because there is no God these statements are always false.

> **Exam tip**
>
> Remember that Mackie is an anti-realist who is also a cognitivist. This makes his theory very different from other anti-realist positions which are non-cognitivist. If relevant you should make this difference clear in the exam.

Ayer's emotivism (non-cognitivist)

REVISED

Moral judgements are neither true nor false

In *Language, Truth and Logic*, Ayer states that his aim is to establish the purpose of philosophical enquiry and ensure philosophers no longer waste their time on disputes which have no foundation and cannot be resolved through a philosophical method. The method Ayer uses is the application of the verification principle (VP), which has its origins in Hume's fork (see **page 98**).

According to Ayer's VP a meaningful proposition is either analytic or synthetic.

● An analytic statement is one that is necessarily true by definition.

● A synthetic statement makes an empirical hypothesis – it tells us what the world is like, and can be empirically verified or falsified.

Ayer's primary target is metaphysics but he also applies the VP to judgements of value, including ethics. When the VP is applied to ethical statements it can be seen that:

● moral judgements are not true by definition

● moral judgements cannot be verified or falsified as there are no facts/ properties in the world which they refer to.

So Ayer is both a non-cognitivist and an anti-realist about moral language. He concludes that moral judgements have no 'factual significance' and that moral concepts such as 'good' and 'right' are mere pseudo-concepts (pseudo means 'by appearance only' or fake). But if moral claims like 'stealing money is wrong' are not genuine propositions (they are not truth-apt), what are they?

> **Revision activity**
>
> Write down three sentences that Ayer would classify as 'meaningful', and three that he would classify as 'meaningless'. Use these in your exam if relevant.

> **Revision activity**
>
> Explain the criticism that the VP fails its own criteria of meaningfulness (see **page 99**).

Moral judgements are expressions of emotion

Ayer, like Hume, connects moral claims with our emotions but Ayer's analysis differs from Hume's.

- For Hume moral terms are *descriptions* of our sympathetic responses to other people's behaviours.
- For Ayer moral terms are *expressions* of emotions, like saying 'boo' (at things we do not like) and 'hooray' (at things we do like), or of attitudes (pro-attitudes and con-attitudes).

So Ayer's theory is a form of emotivism.

Emotivists regards moral judgements as expressive rather than descriptive. These judgements do not point us to facts, but they influence our behaviour by conveying strong feelings of approval or disapproval.

Emotivists have done away with the mysterious moral, non-natural properties that made intuitionism such a strange theory.

Emotivists are also able to explain why it is that moral judgements motivate us ('internalism', see **page 99**) – it is because they express emotion and appeal to emotion, we want to do things that others approve of, and moral judgements motivate us to do exactly that.

> **Key quote**
>
> If I say 'Stealing money is wrong' I produce a sentence with no factual meaning ... It is as if I had written 'Stealing money!!' where the shape and thickness of the exclamation marks show a special sort of moral disapproval.
>
> A.J. Ayer, *Language, Truth and Logic*

Hare's prescriptivism (non-cognitivist)

REVISED

Moral judgements are not descriptive

Richard Hare (1919–2002) continued the debate begun by Moore and Ayer, focusing almost entirely on meta-ethics and the meaning of ethical terms. Hare's theory emerges from emotivism in so far as it further explores how moral judgements are *used* in language, but its prescriptivism is a more complex theory, which differs from both Moore's and Ayer's analysis.

- Hare thinks Moore's open question argument is correct in demonstrating that moral terms like 'good' cannot be defined in naturalistic terms. Hare agrees that any attempt to define moral terms fails – there is always something missing from the definition.
- Hare thinks Moore is wrong in concluding therefore that moral terms describe a non-natural, special, moral property. Hare argues that a careful analysis of moral terms reveals that they are not propositions, making claims about the world, but instead have another *use* in language.

For Hare what characterises value judgements, and in particular moral judgements, is that they commend something; they prescribe for us a course of action.

Moral judgements are prescriptive, universalisable and rational

So Hare, like Ayer, is a non-cognitivist and an anti-realist – he argues that moral judgements are not factual, they do not refer to anything 'out there' in the world, and they cannot be derived from factual premises. Emotivists like Ayer argued that moral judgements are used to *influence* action by expressing approval or disapproval. But prescriptivists like Hare argue that moral judgements *guide* action. So, when carefully analysed, moral judgements can be seen to have several special features according to Hare:

- Moral judgements are prescriptive, so terms like 'good' or 'right' are used to recommend and guide action.
- Moral judgements contain prescriptions/imperatives that are universalisable, so if I say 'lying to the mad axe murderer is wrong' this prescription must be consistently applied by me to everyone in the same situation, including myself in future.
- Moral judgements and discussion are rational (emotivists are wrong to say they are merely expressive) in that:
  - we can ask, and answer, questions about moral conduct
  - we can look for facts that support our moral judgements
  - we can aim for consistency in our moral judgements
  - we can highlight logical contradictions in the moral judgements of others (for example, when they argue that something is bad, and then argue that an identical thing is not bad).

Criticism

Some people are prepared to fully universalise a fanatical prescription, applying it even to themselves. For example, I prescribe that 'Men who are going bald can be harmed without good reason'; and then later accept that 'I am going bald, therefore I can be harmed without good reason'. To be consistent, a prescriptivist should maintain that fanatical prescriptions, which are universalised like this, are just as much moral prescriptions as 'stealing is wrong'. This counter-intuitive implication seems to indicate that prescriptivism is seriously flawed; and Hare's response to this (namely that such fanatics are extremely rare) is weak.

Issues with moral anti-realism

Can moral anti-realism account for how we use moral language?

REVISED

Moral anti-realism arose from an interest in the twentieth century as to the meaning and status of moral terms – the moral realism of Mill and Moore appeared flawed, so Ayer and Hare argued for non-cognitivist, anti-realist positions. However, for moral philosophy to remain relevant it must be tethered to the real world, and it must account for the ways in which moral judgements and values are *used*.

We use moral language every day – it plays a critical role in our personal relationships, our communities, our education system, our business practices, our legal processes, our government policies, and our application of ethics to real-world dilemmas. These uses include:
- moral reasoning and decision-making
- commanding, telling and guiding
- disagreeing and arguing
- persuading and influencing action.

A moral realist (who is also a cognitivist) can account for these uses because there are moral facts about which we are disagreeing or reasoning, or drawing on to make decisions or influence behaviour. But anti-realists and non-cognitivists such as Ayer and Hare struggle to account for these uses.

Uses of moral language	Can emotivism (Ayer) account for these uses?	Can prescriptivism (Hare) account for these uses?
Moral reasoning	**Partly.** Moral judgements are expressions of emotions – approval and disapproval – which are non-rational. But emotivists do allow for rational disputes within morality, but only insofar as these are disagreements over facts.	**Yes.** Moral judgements and discussion are rational in that we can: address questions about moral conduct; find facts that support our moral judgements; aim for consistency and identify the inconsistencies in others.
Commanding and guiding	**No.** Moral judgements are expressions of emotions – they are not commands or prescriptions.	**Yes.** Moral judgements change the behaviour of others through establishing prescriptions that the prescriber thinks we should all follow.
Persuading and influencing	**Yes.** The effect of the emotional content of moral judgements is a psychological one. Expressions of approval like 'good' or 'right' persuade people to behave in a particular way. Likewise expressions of disapproval such as 'wrong' dissuade people from other behaviours.	**Partly.** Moral judgements do aim to change behaviours, not through persuasion but instead through prescription.
Disagreeing and agreeing	**No.** Moral disagreements aren't disagreements about anything – 'she approves of euthanasia but he disapproves of it' is analogous to 'she likes strawberry ice cream but he doesn't' – once the facts have been established, and views expressed, then further disagreement over moral content is not possible.	**Not really.** Consistency and/or universalisability might underpin some disagreements – prescriptivism can account for this. But it cannot explain how an argument can advance from fundamental differences, e.g. you might universalise 'eating meat is wrong' and I might universalise 'eating meat is permissible'.

So emotivism gives a narrow account of the uses of moral judgements: this is limited to persuasion, like advertising. Emotivism faces difficulties in accounting for our other uses of moral language. Moreover we do not always use moral language to influence, for example when talking to people we know already share our views, or who we know don't care about our views.

Prescriptivism gives a broader account of the uses of moral judgements, as rational, universalisable prescriptions setting standards that can be discussed. But Geoffrey Warnock argues that prescriptivism is still too narrow: morality is not always concerned with prescribing – it also is about advising, confessing, resolving etc.

Problem of accounting for moral progress

REVISED

We often compare our moral code with the moral codes of our ancestors, and we judge the past harshly.
- Our ancestors tolerated or approved of practices that we now condemn: slavery, racism, misogyny, human sacrifice etc.
- Our ancestors held a narrow view of what sort of people had moral worth – it was often limited to a small group of people who were 'like them' and they were careless or cruel to those not seen to have moral worth.

Looking back, it is as if our ancestors had a 'moral blind spot' which prevented them from seeing that their practices were cruel, inconsistent or irrational, while our own practices to us appear more inclusive, more consistent, more impartial, less cruel and are improvements on our ancestors' practices. For example:

- We have extended the 'moral circle' to include people of all backgrounds, ethnicities, genders, disabilities.
- We have laws in place to ensure that we treat people equally and fairly, and that we value diversity.
- We have developed 'progressive' moral and legal codes over the past few hundred years, which include:
  ○ the extension of political and voting rights to women
  ○ the abolition of slavery, child labour, corporal punishments (for example, whipping) for crimes
  ○ international laws on the treatment of prisoners of war.

So it is hard not to draw the conclusion that in significant ways our moral codes have got better, our societies have improved and that there has been genuine moral progress.

How might we account for this moral progress? A moral realist can argue that this progress is genuine: that we have become more adept at discovering or embracing those moral facts and properties that exist 'out there'. But moral anti-realists reject mind-independent moral properties and facts. For a moral anti-realist it seems as if we can talk about a *change* in moral codes but cannot speak about 'moral progress'. This is because there is no objective standard we can use to assess whether or not our moral code is an improvement on our ancestors' codes.

But a moral anti-realist can account for improvement or positive progression in other ways.

- A prescriptivist might argue that a society can genuinely improve its *consistency* in universalising its moral judgements (for example, the Romans condemned Celtic human sacrifice, but to be consistent should also have condemned gladiatorial combat).
- A prescriptivist and an emotivist can argue that a society can improve its knowledge of the world, yielding new facts to be considered in moral judgements (for example, Descartes believed that animals cannot feel pain, but biologists have shown that the nervous systems of animals and humans are similar, and this fact has impacted on our treatment of animals).
- An emotivist can argue 'moral progress' just means that we feel more approval for our own moral code than for our ancestral moral codes. As we compare the past and present, our feelings switch from disapproval (for example, child labour and exploitation in the past) to approval (for example, child safeguarding laws in the present).

Does anti-realism become moral nihilism?

Nihilism is the rejection of a particular set of beliefs, and *moral* nihilism is the rejection of morality and its values. Moral nihilists adopt a radical form of scepticism about the possibility of justifying moral principles and judgements. Like moral anti-realists, nihilists argue that there are no moral facts or truths and moral knowledge is not possible. But unlike moral anti-realists, nihilists conclude that if there are no objective values (if they are an invention by different societies, or are merely an expression of emotion or a personal prescription) then morality as a whole is without foundation. Therefore we should abandon our ethical practices and live a life free from the pretence of moral codes.

Revision activity

Explain what moral anti-realism and nihilism have in common. Outline why nihilism could follow as a consequence of anti-realism.

We can distinguish between different types of theories that reject moral facts or properties.

Theory	Agreed	Description	Thinker
Moral anti-realism	No moral facts	We must make some changes in our understanding of what moral terms mean. But with these changes we can continue with our moral behaviours and practices	Ayer/Hare
Moderate moral nihilism	No moral facts	Our understanding of morality is deeply flawed. We must make radical changes in our understanding in order to continue our moral practices	Mackie
Radical moral nihilism	No moral facts	We should abandon our moral practices as they are a sham, and we should live a life free from moral codes	Sartre

The following argument shows how moral anti-realism leads to the more extreme form of moral nihilism.

P1 There are no objective, mind-independent moral facts or properties (moral anti-realism).

P2 If there are no objective moral facts then there is nothing that is morally wrong.

C If there is nothing that is morally wrong then we can do anything we like (moral nihilism).

Moral nihilism might seem more consistent than moral anti-realism – because if there are no moral values then we have no reason or obligation to continue to be moral. For example, Jean-Paul Sartre (1905–80) argued that humans are not defined or bound by anything, that there is no God, and that there are no objective moral values – so we are free to do whatever we like (well, sort of).

Moreover moral anti-realists cannot respond by saying that we 'should' or 'ought to' be moral, since according to their own theory there are no objective moral 'should's or 'ought's.

Criticism

Moral anti-realists who are emotivists or prescriptivists would reject the claim that their position leads to moral nihilism.

- An emotivist can acknowledge that nihilism is not inconsistent with their theory. Within emotivism 'moral wrongness' means an 'expression of disapproval' and it's possible that someone might happen to disapprove (or approve) of nothing at all. But the emotivist might argue this is a rare occurrence, and there is certainly no inevitability to it – most people do disapprove of some things. So P2 is false.

- A prescriptivist (Hare) can also acknowledge that nihilism/amoralism is a position that is logically consistent with prescriptivism – so long as the nihilist rejects all moral judgements and universalises none. But Hare thinks that the risk of nihilism is small: we want to universalise our prescriptions (for example, to tell people what's wrong), and it's often in our interests to do so (for example, to deter them from harming us). So again P2 is false.

Exam checklist

You should be able to:	✓
Outline how moral principles might have their origins in reason, emotion or society	
Explain the distinction between cognitivism and non-cognitivism about ethical language	
Outline and explain how utilitarianism and virtue ethics are forms of moral naturalism	
Explain how intuitionism is a type of non-naturalism	
Explain the issues Moore raises against naturalism:	
• the open question argument	
• the naturalistic fallacy	
Explain the issues raised against moral realist theories (naturalism and non-naturalism):	
• Hume's fork and Ayer's verification principle	
• Hume's argument that moral judgements cannot be beliefs	
• Hume's 'is–ought' gap	
• Mackie's arguments from relativity and from queerness	
Explain what moral anti-realism says about moral judgements	
Explain Mackie's error theory and outline why it is a cognitivist position	
Explain what emotivism claims about the status of moral judgements	
Explain what prescriptivism claims about the status of moral judgements	
Explain the issues raised against moral anti-realist theories:	
• whether moral anti-realism can account for how we use ethical language (e.g. moral reasoning)	
• whether moral anti-realism can account for moral progress	
• whether moral anti-realism becomes moral nihilism	

Glossary

Section 1: Epistemology

Abduction An abductive argument (which is often described as *inference to the best explanation*), is one that proceeds from an effect to argue for the most likely cause.

Anti-realist If you are a realist about something, then you believe that it exists independently of our minds. If you are an anti-realist about something, you think it is mind-dependent. This is closely connected to noncognitivism. For example, in epistemology, anti-realists about perception think that material objects exist only for minds and that a mind-independent world is nonexistent. (Berkeley summed up this idealist position by saying that to be is to be perceived.) An example of anti-realism in religious language is Wittgenstein's theory that religious terms need to be understood within a religious language game.

Apt belief For Ernest Sosa, a belief is an apt one if it is a true one, and is a true one *because* of the cognitive skill of the believer.

Argument An argument is a series of propositions intended to support a conclusion. The propositions offered in support of the conclusion are termed premises.

Belief A state of mind or thought which is about the world. It is a mental representation which claims that something is the case, or that a proposition is true. For example, you may have the belief that Westminster is in London or that cod liver oil is good for your health. A belief will have some degree of evidence in support of it, but is normally regarded as weaker than knowledge, either because knowledge cannot turn out to be false, or because it requires stronger evidence.

Clear and distinct ideas The basic or self-justifying beliefs that Descartes hopes to use as foundations for his system of knowledge. Clear and distinct ideas, we are told, are those which can be 'intuited' by the mind by what he calls the 'light of reason'. In other words, they are truths of reason, truths that can be known with the mind alone. Descartes' examples of clear and distinct ideas are the basic claims of logic, geometry and mathematics. Knowledge of truths of reason, it is claimed, resists any sceptical attack, since we recognise its truth immediately. Our faculty of 'intuition' permits us to recognise the truth without allowing any room for doubt or error. For example, it is in vain to ask how I know that triangles have three sides. Such knowledge is given in the very act of understanding the terms involved. There is no further evidence I need appeal to in order to justify such knowledge.

Cogito Latin for 'I think', and shorthand for Descartes' famous argument to prove his own existence. Descartes attempted to doubt he existed, but realised that in order to doubt this, he must exist. So his own existence was indubitable.

Concept Having a concept of something is what enables one to recognise it, distinguish it from other things and think about it. So if I have the concept of a hedgehog, I can think about hedgehogs, and recognise them when I encounter them, and tell the difference between them and hogs or hedges. Similarly, to have a concept of red is to be able to think about it, recognise it and distinguish it from other colours. According to traditional empiricism, all our concepts are formed as kinds of 'copy' of the original sensations.

Conclusion A statement that comes at the end of an argument and that is supported by the reasons given in the argument. If an argument is sound or valid and all of the premises are true, then the conclusion will also be true.

Deductive argument (also 'a deduction', 'deductively valid' or simply 'valid') An argument where the truth of the conclusion is guaranteed by the truth of the premises. In other words, it is an argument in which the premises entail the conclusion. So if one accepts the truth of the premises, one must, as a matter of logical necessity, accept the conclusion. For example: either you will become a firefighter or a doctor. But you can only become a doctor with a medical degree which you will never get. So you will become a firefighter. A deductive argument is in contrast to an inductive argument.

Direct realism The common-sense view of how perception works. Physical objects have an independent existence in space; they follow the laws of physics and possess certain properties, ranging from size and shape through to colour, smell and texture. When humans are in the presence of such objects under appropriate conditions, they are able to perceive them along with all these properties.

Empiricist Holding an epistemological position that our beliefs and knowledge must be based on experience. David Hume was one philosopher who rigorously applied his empiricist approach to questions in the philosophy of religion.

Epistemology One of the three main areas of philosophical study and analysis. Epistemology, or the theory of knowledge, looks at questions of what it is possible to know, what grounds our claims to knowledge are based on, what is true, what is the distinction between knowledge and belief. (The term is derived from the ancient Greek words, *episteme* meaning 'knowledge', and *logos* meaning 'account' or 'rationale'.)

Evidence The reasons for holding a belief.

Evil demon A device used by Descartes to generate a sceptical argument about the possibility of knowledge of the external world and of basic propositions of arithmetic and geometry. It is conceivable that there exists an extremely powerful spirit or demon bent on deceiving me. If this were the case, then all my perceptions of the world around me could be an illusion produced in my mind by the demon. Even my own body could be a part of the illusion. Moreover, the demon could cause me to make mistakes even about the most simple judgements of maths and geometry, so that I go wrong when adding 2 + 3 or counting the sides of a square.

Evolution The process, described as natural selection by Charles Darwin, by which organisms gradually change over time according to changes in their environment and genetic mutations. Some mutations lead to traits or characteristics which make an organism better suited to an environment and more successful in having offspring that also survive and reproduce; some environmental changes mean that an organism is less suited to its environment and its offspring are less successful in surviving and reproducing. Over long periods of time, and in environmentally stable conditions, the characteristics of an organism become highly adapted to its environment and have all the appearance of being designed for that environment.

External world All that exists outside of or independently of the mind; the physical world.

Fact Something which is the case. For example, it is a fact that the Earth revolves around the Sun.

Forms (theory of) Plato's theory of forms is a theory about types or classes of thing. The word 'form' is used to translate Plato's use of the Greek word 'idea', with which he refers to the type or class to which a thing belongs. Plato argues that over and above the realm of physical objects there is a realm of 'forms' to which individual physical things belong. So in the physical realm there are many tables, but there is also

the single form of the table, the ideal or blueprint of the table, which we recognise not with our senses, but with the mind.

Idea The uses of the word 'idea' are various within the philosophical literature, as well as in ordinary parlance. Here the word is not used in a technical or precise sense, except when in italics where it refers to Locke's use of the word to mean anything of which the mind is conscious, including sense data, concepts and beliefs.

Idealism Idealism as discussed here is an anti-realist theory of perception. Put forward by Berkeley, it is the view that matter does not exist independently of the mind and that all that exists are minds and their ideas. Physical objects are no more than collections of sensations appearing in minds. Objects that are not currently being perceived by any creature are sustained in existence by being perceived in the mind of God.

Indirect realism The view that the immediate objects of perception are sense data or representations and that the physical world is perceived only indirectly via these representations.

Indubitable Not doubtable. A belief which it is not possible to doubt is indubitable.

Inductive Of an argument where the truth of the conclusion is not fully guaranteed by the truth of the premises. For example, moving from particular examples (every raven I have seen has been black) to a generalisation (all ravens are black); or moving from our experience of the past (day has always followed night) to a prediction about the future (day will always follow night). Arguments from analogy are also inductive: they compare two things, and move from what these two things are known to have in common to draw a conclusion about other (unknown) things they are supposed to have in common.

Infallibilism Theory of knowledge which claims that we should only count as knowledge those beliefs that it is impossible to doubt.

Inference The move in an argument from the premises or reasons to the conclusion. For example, in the argument, 'Moriarty had blood on his hands, therefore he must be the murderer', the inference is the move made from the premise that Moriarty had blood on his hands to the conclusion that he is the murderer.

Innate ideas Ideas that exist in the mind which are not acquired from experience. Plato, for example, argued that all ideas or concepts are innate and that the process of acquiring knowledge is not one of learning in the strict sense, but rather of recollecting what we already implicitly know. So we are all born with innate knowledge of the 'forms', and it is this knowledge which enables us to recognise individual exemplars of the forms in this life. Rationalists traditionally favoured the belief that we possess such ideas. Leibniz, for example, argued that such ideas exist implicitly within the mind and that they are brought to the surface of consciousness through experience. Rationalists often use the doctrine of innate ideas to explain the possibility of *a priori* knowledge. Descartes argued that knowledge of mathematics is innate and that the discovery of mathematical truths involves the mind looking into itself to uncover them. Knowledge of the existence of God is also possible, according to Descartes, because we can look into our own mind to discover the idea and deduce his existence in an *a priori* manner, simply through careful mental scrutiny of the idea. Opposed to the doctrine of innate ideas are the empiricists, and in particular John Locke, who devoted the first book of his *Essay Concerning Human Understanding* to their repudiation. Locke argued that all the contents of the mind can be reduced to sensation variously transformed and that the mind at birth is akin to a blank paper.

Insensible/sensible Terms often used by Locke and Berkeley to mean the same as imperceptible and perceptible. For Locke, the minute corpuscles or atoms which compose material objects are 'insensible' because they are too small for us to perceive; whereas the 'sensible' qualities of objects are those we can perceive. For Berkeley, objects consist of sensible qualities alone, for what is insensible does not exist.

Intuition A kind of mental seeing by which rational truths can be recognised. For Descartes, the mind deploys the faculty of intuition when it sees by the 'light of reason' that $2 + 2 = 4$ or that a sphere is bounded by one surface.

Knowledge There are three sorts of knowledge: practical knowledge, knowledge by acquaintance and factual knowledge. The traditional account of factual knowledge claims that it is justified, true belief.

Lemma A subsidiary belief or proposition used to justify or prove another belief/proposition.

Material Made of physical matter. According to Descartes, this involved occupying physical space. In contrast, God is thought of by Christian philosophers as immaterial.

Method of doubt Descartes' sceptical method used to find certainty. Descartes found that many of his beliefs had turned out to be false, and to remedy this situation he elected to cast doubt upon all his beliefs. If any beliefs showed themselves to be indubitable, and could survive the most radical scepticism, then they would have established themselves as absolutely certain. Once he had discovered such beliefs, Descartes hoped to rebuild a body of knowledge based on them which would be free from error.

Necessary/sufficient condition A is a necessary condition for B when you have to have A in order to have B. In other words, if you do not have A, you cannot have B. By contrast, A is a sufficient condition for B when if you have A you must have B too. In other words, having A is enough or sufficient to guarantee that you have B.

Perception The process by which we become aware of physical objects, including our own body.

Predicate Many propositions can be divided into a subject and a predicate, where the subject is the thing that the sentence is about and the predicate gives us information about the subject. For example, in the sentence, 'The balloon is red', the expression 'is red' is the predicate, the term 'balloon' is the subject. Some philosophers argued that in the sentence 'God exists', 'exists' is a predicate applying to 'God'. However, philosophers from Kant onwards have doubted whether existence is a genuine predicate.

Premise Any reason given (usually in the form of a statement or claim) to support the conclusion of an argument.

Primary and secondary qualities According to indirect realism, physical objects have certain primary qualities, such as size and shape, which we are able to perceive. At the same time, we also seem to perceive objects to have a set of secondary qualities, such as colours, sounds and smells. However, these qualities are not actually in the objects themselves, but rather are powers to produce these sensations in us. Such powers are a product of the arrangement of the parts of the object which are too small for us to observe.

Rationalism The tendency in philosophy to regard reason, as opposed to sense experience, as the primary source of the important knowledge of which we are capable. Rationalists are typically impressed by the systematic nature of mathematical knowledge and the possibility of certainty that it affords. Using mathematics as the ideal of how knowledge should be, rationalists typically attempt to extend this type of knowledge into other areas of human inquiry, such as to knowledge of the physical world, or to ethics. Rationalism is traditionally contrasted with empiricism: the view that most of what we know is acquired through experience.

Realism If you are a realist about something, then you believe it exists independently of our minds. If you are an anti-realist about something, you think it is mind-dependent. Examples of realist positions from epistemology are direct realism and indirect realism. What they have in common is the conviction that physical objects are real; that is, that they have an existence independently of our perception of them. See also anti-realism.

Reason The capacity for rational argument and judgement. The process by which we are able to discover the truth of things by pure thought by inferring conclusions from premises. Often contrasted with instinct, emotion or imagination.

Reliabilism A theory of knowledge which claims that the reliability of the (cognitive) process involved in generating a belief is the key factor in whether we should call it knowledge or not. Reliabilism is the claim that knowledge is a true belief that is produced by a reliable process.

Representation In the philosophy of perception, a representation is a sense experience or collection of sense data which appears to picture some aspect of the physical world, such as an object. See also **indirect realism**.

Scepticism Philosophical scepticism entails raising doubts about our claims to know. Global scepticism directs its doubts at all knowledge claims and argues that we can know nothing. Scepticism can also have a more limited application to some subset of our knowledge claims; for example, concerning the possibility of knowledge of the claims of religion or of ethics. The purpose of scepticism in philosophy is first to test our knowledge claims. If they can survive the sceptic's attack, then they may vindicate themselves as genuine knowledge. Descartes used scepticism in this way so that he could isolate a few certainties which he felt could be used as a foundation to rebuild a body of knowledge free from doubt or error. Scepticism is also used as a tool for distinguishing which types of belief can be treated as known and which cannot, thereby delimiting those areas where knowledge is possible. In this way, philosophers often exclude certain regions of human enquiry as fruitless, since they cannot lead to knowledge. Empiricists, for example, often argue that knowledge of religious claims is impossible since they cannot be verified in terms of experience.

Self What the word 'I' refers to. The essence of the person and what many philosophers, most notably Descartes, have argued we are directly aware of through introspection.

Sensation The subjective experience we have as a consequence of perceiving physical objects, including our own bodies, such as the experience of smelling a rose or of feeling hungry.

Sense data What one is directly aware of in perception. The subjective elements which constitute experience. For example, when perceiving a banana, what I actually sense is a collection of sense data: the way the banana seems to me, including a distinctive smell, a crescent-shaped yellow expanse, a certain texture and taste. According to sense data theorists, we make judgements about the nature of the physical world on the basis of immediate awareness of these sense data. So, on the basis of my awareness of the sense datum of a yellow expanse, plus that of a banana smell, and so on, I judge that I am in the presence of a banana. In this way, we build up a picture of the physical world, and so all empirical knowledge can rest on the foundation of sense data.

Sense impressions The colours, noises, tastes, sounds and smells that one is aware of when perceiving the world. Also known as sense data.

Sensible See **insensible/sensible**.

Solipsism The view that all that can be known to exist is my own mind. This is not normally a position defended by philosophers, but rather a sceptical trap into which certain ways of thinking appear to lead. For example, if it is urged that all that can be truly known is what one is directly aware of oneself, then it follows that one cannot know anything of which one is not directly aware. This might include the minds of other people (which one can only learn about via their behaviour), or, more radically, the very existence of the physical world, including one's own body (which one can only learn about via one's sense experience of it).

Sufficient condition See **necessary/sufficient condition**.

Theory of forms See **forms**.

Veridical Truthful or accurate. Perception is veridical if it is faithful to reality, and for indirect realists this means it provides an accurate representation of the external world. Veridical perceptions contrast with hallucinations or illusions where the representation of reality is inaccurate or misleading.

Virtue epistemology This is a recent approach to the thinking about the concept of knowledge. It claims that we should seek to define knowledge as the true beliefs that have been brought about through sound cognitive processes (for example, epistemic virtues such as careful reasoning or clear vision) and where the beliefs are true ones *because* of the epistemic virtues that brought them about.

Section 2: Moral philosophy

Agency The capacity of an agent to act in any given environment.

Agent A being who is capable of action. Agency and action are typically restricted to human beings, because human beings have the capacity to reason, make a choice between two courses of action, then do what they have chosen.

Anti-realism See **moral realism and anti-realism**.

Applied ethics Like normative ethics, this is also a type of 'first-order' theory. It looks at the application of ethical theories to concrete situations and moral dilemmas that people face, such as abortion, euthanasia and the treatment of animals.

Argument from analogy Arguments which compare two things and draw a conclusion about one of them on the basis of their similarities are called arguments from analogy, or analogical arguments.

Autonomy (from the Greek *auto* – self, and *nomos* – law) An agent has autonomy insofar as it is rational and free. For Kant, moral autonomy was only achieved through following the categorical imperative.

Autonomy of ethics See **is–ought gap**.

Categorical imperative See **imperative**.

Cognitivism and non-cognitivism Cognitivism in ethics is the view that moral judgements are propositions which can be known – they refer to the world and they have a truth-value (they are capable of being true or false). Non-cognitivism is the view that moral judgements cannot be known, because they do not say anything true or false about the world (they do not have a truth-value). There are many different forms of non-cognitivism, such as emotivism, prescriptivism and nihilism. See also **realism and anti-realism**.

Consequentialist ethics A type of normative moral theory which views the moral value of an action as lying in its consequences. So an action is judged to be good if it brings about beneficial consequences, and bad if it brings about harmful ones. This is in contrast to deontological ethics. Egoism and utilitarianism are two examples of consequentialism.

Deontological ethics A type of normative moral theory that views the moral value of an action as lying in its dutiful motives. Generally, deontologists (such as Kant) propose certain rules, bound by duties, which guide us as to which actions are right and which are wrong. This is in contrast to consequentialism. Kantian ethics is an example of a deontological theory.

Descriptive See **prescriptive and descriptive**.

Disposition Our tendency to behave in certain ways, our character traits. This term is used by virtue ethicists, who believe we ought to develop virtuous dispositions.

Duty An action which we are required or impelled to carry out. Kant's deontological theory places duty at its centre. For Kant, duties are experienced as imperatives.

Emotivism A non-cognitivist theory of the meaning of moral terms and judgements. In its basic form, emotivism claims that moral judgements do not refer to anything in the world, but are expressions of feelings of approval or disapproval.

Error theory An anti-realist theory of ethical language put forward by J.L. Mackie. It proposes that our moral judgements are making objective claims about the world (so it is a cognitivist position), but these claims are always false (there is nothing 'out there' in the world which our moral terms actually refer to).

Ethics See **Moral philosophy**.

Eudaimonia According to many ancient Greek philosophers, *eudaimonia* is the goal or 'good' we are all striving for. Sometimes translated as 'happiness', it is probably closer in meaning to 'flourishing'. Aristotle's virtue ethics is centred around *eudaimonia*.

Fallacy This refers to an argument which has gone wrong, either because a mistake has been made, rendering the argument invalid; or because the argument has a form, or structure, which is always invalid (see also the naturalistic fallacy).

Good Actions are good according to whether they bring about certain positive outcomes – these may be pleasure or happiness, or something more intangible (Moore believed that love of friendship and beauty were goods). Consequentialists believe that moral value lies in the good (or bad) consequences of an action. But 'good' also has a functional meaning, in the sense that 'good' means 'fulfilling your function well'. Aristotle believed that we had a function and hence could be good in both senses: by being good (fulfilling our function) we could reach the good (*eudaimonia*).

Good will For Kant, a good will is one that acts for the right reason (which means following rules that you could rationally will that everyone else should follow too). A good will is the only thing that is good without qualification.

Hedonism The claim that pleasure is the good. Many utilitarians are hedonists, in that they believe we ought to try to maximise pleasure (for the majority).

Hume's law See **is–ought gap**.

Hypothetical imperative See **imperative**.

Imperative In Kantian ethics we experience our duties as commands (imperatives) which are categorical, or absolute. These categorical imperatives are commands that we are obliged to follow no matter what, and according to Kant, only these are moral imperatives. As rational agents we can work out the categorical imperative by asking whether the maxim that lies behind our action is universalisable. Other imperatives, things we should do in order to achieve some goal, are conditional or hypothetical imperatives, and they are not moral according to Kant.

Intuitionism A realist theory which claims that we can determine what is right or good according to our moral intuitions. For intuitionists, the terms 'right' and 'good' do refer to something objective, but they cannot be reduced to naturalistic terms.

Is-ought gap Hume argued that we cannot draw a conclusion which is evaluative (containing 'ought') from premises which are purely factual or descriptive. To some philosophers this indicated the autonomy of ethics, that is, that the ethical realm was entirely distinct from other, factual or naturalistic, realms.

Judgement A moral judgement is a decision made (in advance or retrospectively) about the rightness or goodness of a course of action (our own or someone else's) or, for virtue theorists, of someone's character.

Kantian ethics A deontological ethical theory developed by or influenced by Kant. At the heart of Kantian ethics is the claim that we can determine what is right, and what our duties are, through the categorical imperative.

Liberty Political liberty is the freedom you have to perform acts which are not prohibited by the state. The more actions that a government prohibits through law, the less political liberty you have.

Maxim A rule underlying our actions. For example, in stealing £10 from your mum's wallet, you would (perhaps unconsciously) be acting on a rule like this: 'When I need money, I will take it from my parents without telling them.'

Meta-ethics Sometimes called 'second-order ethics', this is the study by moral philosophers of the meaning of moral judgements. This covers issues such as realism/antirealism, cognitivism/non-cognitivism, the is-ought gap, the naturalistic fallacy, and the objectivity/subjectivity of moral judgements.

Moral philosophy The philosophical study of our ideas of moral good, of how to live and of the status of moral judgements.

Moral realism and moral anti-realism Moral realists believe that in some sense moral terms refer to something real – for example, pleasure, happiness, utility, the moral law or God's command. So, from a realist position, morality is discovered. Moral anti-realists believe that moral terms do not refer to anything real, but are something else entirely – for example, expressions of feelings (emotivism), prescriptions to other people (prescriptivism) or they refer to nothing at all (nihilism). See also **cognitivism and non-cognitivism**.

Naturalism The view that we can explain moral concepts, such as good, in naturalistic terms, such as happiness or pleasure.

Naturalistic fallacy G.E. Moore attacked naturalism because he claimed that it committed a fallacy, namely of trying to define the indefinable. Moore believed that moral terms such as good could not be defined (he held they were non-natural), and that naturalists tried to define them in naturalistic terms. He particularly singled out the utilitarians in his attack.

Nihilism An extreme scepticism about the possibility of knowledge of moral values. It is the state of having no values, or the rejection of morality in its conventional form, or the belief that values are groundless or illusory.

Non-cognitivism See **cognitivism and non-cognitivism**.

Normative ethics Sometimes called 'first-order ethics', this term covers moral theories that offer action-guides. These are rules, principles or standards by which we make moral judgements, and according to which our conduct is directed. There are three general forms of normative theory: deontological, consequentialist and virtue ethics.

Partiality Humans almost universally have a special interest in ourselves and in those people closest to us; we value them more highly and tend to favour them above the interests of others – this is partiality. Moral theories such as utilitarianism require that we take an impartial stance, and value our own interests, and the interests of those close to us, and the interests of strangers all equally. Virtue ethics does not require impartiality, and claims to be able to account for partiality within a consistent moral system.

Person In ordinary language, this refers to human beings, but recently some philosophers have asked what is special about persons and whether a) all human beings are persons and b) some non-human beings might count as persons. The sorts of qualities that characterise persons might include agency, autonomy, rationality, self-consciousness, and so on.

Preference utilitarianism This is the theory which claims that an action is good according to the number of preferences it fulfils. An action is bad if it goes against the majority of (relevant) people's preferences. The strength of preferences may also be taken into account. See also utilitarianism.

Prescriptive and descriptive A prescriptive statement is one that guides action; it tells us what to do. A descriptive statement, on the other hand, simply tells us the way things are.

Prescriptivism A non-cognitivist view of the meaning of moral terms and judgements. Like emotivists, prescriptivists believe that moral language has a special use, but they believe that the purpose of moral judgements is to prescribe actions, in other words to urge others to act in a certain way.

Proposition A sentence that makes a claim about the way the world actually is. Non-cognitivists such as the emotivists claim that moral judgements are not propositions; in other words, they are not making claims about the world and are neither true nor false.

Realism/anti-realism See **moral realism and moral anti-realism**.

Relativism Moral relativism is the view that moral judgements vary according to (are relative to) the social context in which they are made. So, moral values or standards of conduct are different in different societies: what is right for you may not be right for me, and so on.

Right Actions are right according to whether they ought to be done, irrespective of the particular situation, or the consequences that result from a course of action. Deontological theorists believe that moral value lies solely in what is right (rather than in what is good) and that we have obligations or duties to do what is right. However, consequentialist theorists are quite happy to redefine 'right' to mean 'actions that bring about the good'.

Rights A right is an entitlement that I have to the protection of certain powers, interests or privileges. It is debatable whether we can have rights only because we make a contract within society, or whether we have 'natural rights' which exist independently of any contract. Rights may be seen as the converse of duties; thus if I have a right to X, then you have a duty to promote X or at least not interfere in my access to X.

Statement See **proposition**.

Teleological Purpose, goal or end, deriving from the Greek word *telos*. A teleological ethical theory is one that says we should be striving to achieve certain moral goals – for Aristotelians this would be virtue; for utilitarians the goal would be happiness. See also consequentialist ethics.

Universalisable A fundamental feature of most ethical theories. A principle is universalisable if it is applied to all people equally and in the same way. Some philosophers (including prescriptivists) have seen this as part of the very meaning of a moral judgement – it applies to everyone in the same situation. Consequentialists (Bentham and Mill), deontologists (Kant) and even existentialists (Sartre) have all appealed to universalisability at some point in their theories. For Kantians, the principle of universalisability has to be a more rigorous version of the golden rule: it says that we should only act on those rules which we can will to be universal laws (that is, without contradiction or inconsistency).

Utilitarianism A consequentialist moral theory, perhaps inspired by Hume (although he is closer to virtue ethics) and developed first by Bentham and then by Mill and Sidgwick. In most of its forms it is a hedonistic theory claiming that what is good (that is, what we ought to strive to bring about) is as much pleasure or happiness as possible for the majority of people. In its negative forms, it says we ought to strive to reduce pain or harm to the majority of people.

Utility Welfare or use for the majority of people. For Bentham and Mill, utility came to mean 'pleasure' or 'happiness'.

Verification principle The rule put forward by verificationists that a proposition is only meaningful if it can be verified either empirically (shown to be true or false by experience/observation) or by analysis of the meanings of the terms involved (through being true or false by definition).

Vice In Aristotelian virtue ethics, a vice is a character trait or disposition which is to be avoided as it prevents us from flourishing (for the ancient Greeks, it is a flaw). It is the opposite of virtue. Common vices include dishonesty, lack of compassion, cowardice, selfishness, indulgence and not revising for philosophy exams.

Virtue A character trait or disposition which is to be valued (for the ancient Greeks, it is a disposition which is excellent). Common virtues include wisdom, courage, self-control, honesty, generosity, compassion, kindness.

Virtue ethics A normative ethical theory which locates value not in an action or its consequences, but in the agent performing the act. Virtue ethicists stress the need to develop virtuous dispositions, and to judge actions within the broader context of what someone is inclined to do. So a person may be judged to be virtuous or vicious through noting how they are disposed to act. Frustratingly, for many people, virtue ethicists fail to give us a formula (unlike consequentialists and deontologists) that guides us in what we ought to do in any particular situation.